THE OPEN CLASSROOM:

A Practical Guide for the Teacher of the Elementary Grades

by

ROSE SABAROFF

and

MARY ANN HANNA

The Scarecrow Press, Inc.
Metuchen, N.J.   1974

Library of Congress Cataloging in Publication Data

Sabaroff, Rose Epstein.
  The open classroom.

  Includes bibliographical references.
  1. Open plan schools—Handbooks, manuals, etc.
I. Hannna, Mary Ann, joint author. II. Title.
LB1029.06S22   372.1'3   74-6442
ISBN 0-8108-0726-2

TABLE OF CONTENTS

INTRODUCTION

Educators throughout America today are advocating open classrooms as an alternative to our present educational system. Designers are leaving walls out of new schools so that open space will be available. Yet few schools and universities have begun to train teachers in techniques of open education; and those which have are turning out only a small percentage of the teaching staff in America today. In-service teachers and administrators in our schools were predominantly educated in a traditional system. These traditional educational values were instilled, consciously or unconsciously, during the early years of training; and educators who desire to move to an open classroom environment must make a conscious attempt to develop values in line with open education.

Many educators do value the advantages of open education for our youth today and would like to learn how to open their own classrooms. They realize the need to develop students who are thinking, resourceful, responsible individuals. Yet, open classrooms cannot be easily implemented after a casual reading of the theory of the open classroom. Readers who wish to initiate an open classroom face a process of changing their traditional attitudes toward children and children's traditional attitudes toward both children and teachers.

The open classroom is often thought of as an open

1

space, created by removing walls between classrooms. However, the open classroom really starts in the openness of the teacher's outlook. To open a classroom, a teacher must start by considering:

> Does all knowledge emanate from a teacher talking from the front of the class to a group of children?
>
> Who besides herself can help children learn?
>
> What materials and activities besides the approved texts can be used in teaching?
>
> Does learning take place when the teacher presents information, or does learning require that the learner engage positively in an activity selected to ensure that learning?
>
> Does trust between teacher and pupil facilitate learning?
>
> Can children take an active role in their own learning?

Teachers and children alike must learn to become open with one another and trust each other. The following thoughts on creating an open environment may be helpful as a prelude to a discussion of how the average class and teacher can make the transition from traditional to open classroom:

L   Open education takes place in a relaxed educational environment in which maximum trust is developed between teacher and students; in which each person (students & teachers) is regarded as a human being with specific rights. It is within such a framework that the teacher directs the children toward meeting the educational objectives of the curriculum. However, she also considers a variety of learning activities and selects those that will best meet the emotional, physical, and social needs of each child as well. \

The way space is used also reflects the openness of the environment. Chairs in straight lines where children only see the backs of each other's heads do not provide the learning possibilities that other arrangements of the classroom might afford: children sitting face-to-face in twos, threes, or small groups, helping each other meet the objectives. (More specifics will be given later--see Chapter 1.)

Many books have been written which expound the theories of open education and which research the history of open education both in America and Great Britain. These are all of value to the teacher about to embark upon the venture of open education. However, this book's purpose is to supplement such background reading with a workable plan for helping a teacher who desires to move toward open education. The word "desires" is of utmost importance. A teacher must believe that children can play an active role in their own learning and that a variety of activities can be arranged to further that learning. If not, the teacher does not possess the basic requirements for moving toward open education.

The following sequence for transforming a traditional classroom into an open environment is a highly structured one. When an open environment has finally been achieved, the teacher may no longer be restricted to such definite time limits. However, during the transition period a schedule will enable the teacher to budget time so that all subjects and all students receive adequate attention. Once students and teacher have learned to work responsibly in an open environment, scheduling of time can become more flexible.

Chapter 1

TEACHER ATTITUDES AND THE OPEN ENVIRONMENT

All teachers want to be successful in their teaching,
to see measurable change in their pupils in the direction of
the curriculum's objectives. The open classroom does not
assume that children can achieve the school's educational
objectives without the guidance and aid of the teacher. Al-
though we expect children to be more active participants in
their learning, we expect teachers to create and select the
appropriate materials or activities with which the children
will interact.

If a teacher and a class are to succeed in an open
classroom, the following attitudes must be developed.

I. ✗ The teacher is responsible for maintaining an environment in which active learning can occur.

The teacher must define the educational objectives
which she wishes her children to achieve--and here we mean
daily, weekly, yearly behavioral objectives. The open classroom concept does not presuppose that children will do whatever they feel like doing. Rather, it asks children to help
themselves and each other in a more active and satisfying
way to meet the behavioral objectives prescribed by the
school's curriculum. The teacher will select the materials
and activities which will best engage the full participation

4

of each child. ✗

Teaching, to be successful for all children in a class, must be diagnostic-prescriptive; that is, the teacher sets objectives for teaching each small group and, as the teaching proceeds, keeps a record of each child's errors. This is on-the-spot, continuous <u>diagnosis</u>. For the follow-up after the lesson, activities are then <u>prescribed</u> for that small group which will reinforce the objectives. In addition, specific assignments are made for each child, according to the errors he has made. Errors must not accumulate; they must be worked on and eliminated on a daily basis. Therefore, the materials and activities that go into a learning center reflect what the teacher has planned and prescribed for each individual in the group as well as for the group as a whole. Until a teacher knows the children well, plans must provide for the follow-up of every possible type of error. Gradually, it is possible to anticipate what errors are likely to occur or what specific learning may cause difficulty, and to plan the reinforcement that will be needed. Some items in the center may thus change on a day-to-day basis; others may be used by different children on different days. Some items will be for individuals, some for use in pairs, others for group use. But always, the materials in the learning center reflect the objectives of the lesson being taught to a group. Paraprofessionals, if available, can be most helpful in working with children as they interact with materials and activities in the learning centers.

As plans are developed for each group, the teacher must consider each individual's needs. Unlike the traditional classroom teacher, the teacher in the open classroom cannot make one plan for the class as a whole, or one which is designed for presentation to only three ability groups.

Consideration must be given to individual interests, individual needs, individual attention spans, and individual learning rates so as to provide the potential for learning success for each child.   Planned activities must be inclusive enough to meet both individual and group requirements.

Even in an open environment, group instruction is valid and necessary, but the open classroom teacher will be careful to vary the means of instruction so as to reach all children.   If instruction is geared to individual needs, then teaching of small groups with individual follow-up will predominate.   There may, however, be situations in which large group instruction will be valid, such as a creative writing lesson, an introductory science lesson, a social studies film, etc.

During instructional periods, the teacher in an open classroom still has the responsibility to see that children receive instruction in the basic skills of reading and mathematics.   The acquisition of these two basic skills is necessary if the child is to become an independent learner.   Individualized follow-up must be provided to insure success for each child on a daily basis.

II. The teacher is responsible for promoting conditions conducive to learning.

These conditions go far beyond the physical arrangement of the classroom.   An attractive, stimulating, orderly classroom which constantly changes to provide for the needs of children is important, but the teacher also has the responsibility for setting the emotional tone of the classroom.

Self-confidence is highly related to the child's ability to learn and to make important decisions concerning his learning.   The teacher should therefore be careful to conduct

the classroom in such a way that each child meets certain
measures of success and feels that he has the ability to
learn.   Children also perform best in an atmosphere which
is non-threatening, and the teacher must build trust between
the children and herself.   Lines of communication must be
kept open so that children will feel free to express themselves.

Following are five suggestions for assuring a less
threatening environment for children: 1) Use a quiet, confident tone of voice; 2) Give directions in as few words as
possible, and make them specific, not general.   For young
children, give only one direction at a time, and make sure
they have understood and followed this direction before giving
another; 3) Give the child enough time to answer a question
or complete an activity; 4) Make positive rather than negative suggestions; for example, to call the children's attention, the teacher might say, "Look up, let me see your
eyes," rather than "Keep quiet"; 5) Greet each child at the
door first thing in the morning, make a pleasant remark,
direct him to an activity--in short, help start the day
happily.

Children also learn best by being allowed to manipulate concrete materials.   A wide variety of such materials
should be available.   One caution: when children are allowed
always to choose the materials they wish to work with, they
may tend to choose those with which they are already familiar.   The teacher should gradually direct children toward
other activities of educational value, and help them develop
new interests.   The teacher should remember that learning
takes place whenever a child is fully involved.   If interaction with a new material or concept brings success, this
now becomes part of a child's interest repertoire.   Thus the

teacher, a paraprofessional, or someone must be there to
help the child overcome obstacles.

Children are also good teachers.   When a child is
excited about something he has learned, he will want to
share it with someone.   Allow children opportunities to do
so.   Children who have like interests will often want to
work together on learning projects.   This is fine, but the
way the teacher initiates new pairing of children can contribute to new interest developments.

III.   The teacher is responsible for acting as a humanizing
       agent and transforming the classroom into a community.

The teacher in an open classroom must think of adults
and children as human beings.   Each person is to be treated
as a person worthy of consideration.   Nevertheless, the role
of teacher to pupil is an adult-child relationship, and children will not respect an adult who tries to become one of
them.   Children want an adult to care about them as individuals and guide their development.

The teacher must consider that when a child is requested to perform some task, it is a task worth performing.   The teacher should also review each task to be sure
that it is one which the child can do successfully, yet one
which will expand his experiences.

The teacher should regard each child as a person, not
as an object to be manipulated, and must help the children
realize that each person in the classroom has individual
worth and deserves respect.   If the teacher gives each
child equally respectful attention and accepts each child's
differences, the children will do likewise.

A realistic approach to humanizing the classroom is
for the teacher and the children to look upon their classroom

as a community in which they live and work and play.   The
rights of each person should be understood.   The reasons
for rules and regulations should be discussed.   Each person
should strive to make the community one in which the atmosphere is trusting, communicative, stimulating and workable.   This will be achieved only through joint cooperation
of all participants.   It cannot be achieved if the teacher is
too domineering.   The teacher, nevertheless, must guide
and facilitate the gradual growth of the community.   This is
not a concept which will be developed in a few days.   The
following guide for achieving a transition to an open classroom, it is hoped, will help the teacher and children develop the necessary attitudes.

PART I

THE FIRST PHASE

Chapter 2

THE FIRST TWO WEEKS

For a person who has taught in a traditional classroom for any length of time, beginning the day in a free
and open manner can be a disheartening experience. Most
traditional teachers use the beginning of the day, when the
children are quietly in their seats performing assigned tasks,
as a moment to collect themselves, to take the role, to
perform other duties required by the administration, and
to prepare materials to be used in the morning's work.
Some teachers may be apprehensive about what children may
do during the rest of the day if they are allowed to move
around freely in the morning. This apprehension can gen-
erate failure if attempts at opening the classroom are tried
in the beginning hours of the school day. The early hours
of the afternoon session, the period following lunch, can
provide a more relaxing and normal beginning for the teacher who wishes to make the transition to an open environment.

The Story Hour

The most important principle underlying open education is a complete feeling of trust that acts as a bond of
communication between pupils and teacher. One small change

13

in the physical arrangement of the classroom and a minor
change in the day's schedule can be the first step toward
developing pupil-teacher trust.   Ideally, the teacher can
bring into the classroom any available old rug, large
enough for all the pupils and the teacher to gather for a
thirty-minute story hour following the lunch period.   If
obtaining and placing a rug in the classroom is not feasible,
several other possibilities are available.   Children may bring
sample rug squares, easily obtained from carpet stores, and
those who wish may be allowed to stretch out on the floor;
others may prefer chairs.   The important thing is that this
should all take place in a corner of the room and promote
a feeling of togetherness.   A shelf of library books may be
placed in this corner to encourage individual reading during
the day.   If the weather and surroundings permit, at least
some of the story hours may take place outside under a
tree.   Even if story hours have previously been part of
the day, relaxing on the rug will promote a casual feeling of
closeness and communication, perhaps not present before.
The first day of this innovation must be greeted with enthusiasm on the part of the teacher.   The students must
feel that this story period is a reward, and a result of the
teacher's trust in their ability to conduct themselves.   A
workable plan for this thirty-minute period follows:

> First 20 minutes: an exciting story or story sequel to
> be read by the teacher.

> Last 10 minutes: a relaxing discussion about the story
> and what it makes a person think of,
> things the children like, the weather,
> etc.   The key word here is relaxing,
> so that the children begin to think of
> the teacher as someone who is human.

It is important during the first day of story time that

the teacher sit on the floor with the class or in a small
chair, thus becoming one of them. Most children of elementary age will take sitting on the rug as a great treat.
However, if some children protest that they cannot sit on
the floor, let them pull chairs over to the edge of the rug.
This will probably only last a few days after they realize
that the teacher is going to sit on the rug with them.   It
is also important that story-time be an everyday occurrence.
If something prevents it from occurring at the regularly
scheduled time, make sure that it happens as soon as possible after the interruption.

The Expanded Story Hour

After one week of the above schedule, pupils and
teacher will normally be ready for slight changes in the
story-time.   The first five to ten minutes of the period
should be used by the teacher to praise something which has
occurred in the classroom during the morning. For example:
"Bob, I really liked the way you stuck with your reading
work today until you were finished.   Susan, I liked the way
you helped Mary find her page when you came to the reading
group.   I wonder if some of you could tell me some things
that you think were very good about our morning."   This last
statement allows the children to become part of the interaction, which will help build self-confidence.   Following
this discussion, allow a child to read a story to the group--
if your class has sufficient reading ability for even the
simplest story.   If you are dealing with a beginning first
grade or a kindergarten, you might allow some of the children to tell a favorite story during this period.

At this point, variety is necessary to keep the story

hour from becoming a routine which is accepted but not
looked forward to.   One day might be for children to read
or tell stories, or the teacher might read a new exciting
book.   Another day might be for a flannel-board story told
by the teacher; another might include a story filmstrip shown
against the wall above the rug where all are seated; and another day might even including the telling of favorite ghost
stories.

The closing few minutes of story-time can be used
to make suggestions for the afternoon period.   It is important
to begin these suggestions at this time so that the children
will accept it as routine when you begin to extend your open
period into the afternoon.   The following is an example of
what is said: "You know, this morning I was upset by the
noise that some people were making when I was trying to
give the class instructions on how to complete your math
pages. I hope that this afternoon all of you will try to help
your friends in the room by being quiet enough so that they
will all be able to hear.   Do you think we could try that
this afternoon?"   Following this, brief instructions about
what is to be done next in the day's schedule could be presented.

Chapter 3

THE THIRD THROUGH SIXTH WEEKS

After two or three weeks of the extended story-time, children and teacher should be ready to move into a short afternoon activity period. It is most important, however, that the teacher feel comfortable and confident about this move before beginning it. The teacher should feel that she knows each child as an individual, and that each child looks forward to story-time and is involved in it. The teacher must also feel accepted as an individual by the children. If more time is required to reach this attitude, it should certainly be taken.

Beginning the Short Afternoon Activity Period

The afternoon activity period should be introduced at the end of story-time and will require a great deal of pre-planning on the part of the teacher if it is to be successful. At the beginning, the activity period may last only forty-five minutes to one hour. Later, it will be extended to include the entire afternoon. It is best to plan five activities and break the class down into five groups. In a class with an enrollment of 25-30, this allows small working groups of 5-6 children each. Each group should complete one activity each day and rotate through all five during the week. Thus, the

planning of five activities will last all week and take the
place of five class activities which the teacher may have
used in the past.   Initially, children will be assigned to the
groups and the activities.   This is important for several
reasons: 1) it allows the teacher the security of knowing
that each child has completed all the activities and that no
one child is being left out; 2) it prevents the confusion that
can occur when children are given total freedom to select
an activity for the first time; 3) it gives the children the
chance to learn that they have a responsibility to complete
certain amounts of work before going on to other activities;
4) and finally, it allows the children to experience various
activities in rotation during the week rather than staying too
long with one activity.

Activities should be planned so that at least three or
four of them can be completed with little teacher supervision.
The following example is a plan for five groups:

Group A: If the behavioral objective is to help the children
become aware of persons in the community who
help their family, then the following activity might
be appropriate.
Distribute to each child a large piece of paper
and several magazines.   Across the top of the
paper, the child will print or the teacher will
have printed beforehand the inscription, PEOPLE
WHO HELP MY FAMILY.   Brief directions should
be given telling the children that there are people
in the community who help our families and the
children are asked to name one or two.   Their
assignment is to look through the magazines and
find pictures of people who are such helpers and

to paste the pictures on the piece of paper. If
the children have writing skills they should label
each picture.

Group B: If the behavioral objective is to allow the children
to experience creative free movement to a specific selection of music, then the following activity
might be appropriate.

(A record player will be needed for this activity,
and if possible also have earphones available. If
the earphones are not available in your school,
place the record player in a corner and lower the
volume.)

Give each child a 9 x 12 piece of paper (or similar size) and a black crayon. Place a light selection of instrumental music on the record player
and have each child make scribbles in time to the
music for several minutes. Stop the record and
instruct the children to take various colored crayons and color inside of the scribbles to produce
a stained-glass effect.

Group C: If the behavioral objective is to help the children
become aware of the sequence of events, try the
following activity. Give each child three or four
newspaper cartoons which have been cut apart.
(Be sure to keep each set bound by a paper clip
or rubber band so that different cartoon strips are
not mixed.) Direct each child to put the cartoons
in what he feels is the correct order, and to paste
the cartoon pieces on the paper given him. When
he has finished, he is to create some cartoons of
his own. Neither the teacher nor the child should

worry about how well a child can draw.   The
teacher should tell them that the funnier the draw-
ings, the sillier the cartoons will be.

Group D: If the behavioral objective is to make the children
more aware of similar objects placed in the same
category, then the teacher might choose to use the
following activity.

Several large jars containing a large variety of
beans are placed on a desk or a table.   Each
child is given an egg carton and is asked to sort
the beans into the carton--one type of bean in
each section.   When they finish they are to take
a piece of oak tag paper that is provided and to
paste the largest bean at the top and decrease in
size down to the smallest bean.   (This will be
their work to take home.)

Group E: In order to begin to develop independent working
skills in the children, the teacher might choose
as a behavioral objective, helping the children
become proficient in operating a cassette tape
recorder.

This will be the group that will require most of
the teacher's attention during the activity period.
Bring a small cassette tape recorder into the
classroom.   The first few minutes should be
spent explaining the operation of the recorder.
Next, inform the group that they are going to be
taped.   Take a familiar story such as the "Three
Bears" and assign each a part, being sure to include a narrator.   Illustrate the parts as follows:
"Once there were three bears.   Let's ask each

bear to say hello." Now each person takes part.
"One day Mama bear fixed porridge, but when
Baby bear went to eat his, it was too hot and so
was Mama's and Poppa's. So they went for a
walk. In a little while Goldilocks came to visit."
Now Goldilocks takes her part. Help them pass
the microphone around the group. When the story
is completed, play it back so that the group can
hear. If time permits, let them do another. As
each child takes his turn recording, the teacher
may use the time to work among the other groups
to make sure their work is progressing successfully. Facility in use of the recorder will be an
important skill for each child as the classroom
becomes more open.

The pupils should be made to understand that each of
them will get a chance to do all of the activities some time
during the week. The teacher should have all the materials
prepared and organized, so that they can be handed to each
group as they begin work. Make sure that each child knows
the teacher trusts him to act in a responsible manner, and
that he is so smart that he can do this work on his own
without the teacher's attention. The five specific activities
outlined above are only examples--each teacher should select
and design appropriate activities which will reflect both the
interests of the children and the behavioral objectives to be
achieved. Children will need to be instructed in the use of
the phonograph, tape recorder or any other equipment or
materials before they are asked to use it in a group on their
own.

Make getting into the grouped arrangement a game.
For instance, have the children sit on the rug and close

their eyes. Tell them that when you tap them they are to
follow you. Process one group at a time, giving that group
its directions. Then return for another group. Make sure
that directions are concise and clear, so that only a minute
need be taken with each group. If you have a child who
causes disruption, have him stay with your group but not
participate in it. Only a few days of non-participation is
needed (when activities are fun) before children learn what
type of behavior is acceptable and will allow them to participate. Depending on the character of the class, positive
reinforcement may be used at the end of the activity period;
for example, a piece of candy or a star to all children who
worked well.

The Clean-Up Period

Clean-up is an important habit to instill in all members of the class, including the teacher, from the very first
day. The most important aspect of clean-up is maintaining
a consistent degree of cleanliness from day to day; the
teacher should never say that tomorrow they will do a more
thorough job. Good clean-up procedures must be taught
from the beginning. Each individual should be responsible
for cleaning-up after his or her activity; every article should
be returned to the place from which it was taken. At the
outset, the teacher might find it helpful to reward individuals
with a piece of candy, a star, or a "good worker" label,
etc., when they have cleaned-up nicely. If the habit of
cleaning-up is instilled in the first week, it will not become
a problem as the open atmosphere grows. It is advantageous to devise a signal to let the children know when the
activity period is almost over so that cleaning up can begin.

The signal should be used from the very first day.   An excellent signaling device is a record of marches or other favorite songs of the class since it will allow an adequate time (up to 10 minutes) while providing a pleasant background.

Altering the Short Activity Period
to Allow Choice of Activities

The short activity period should be used for at least two weeks, ending on or about the fourth week.   The groups should be rotated among activities each day so that by the end of the week they will have experienced the full variety of activities.   Each day the teacher will spend most of her time with one group, the group which requires the most teacher direction or the one to which a new activity is being introduced.   At the beginning of the fifth week, a slight change in the approach will move the class a step closer to openness.   At this point, the teacher should plan four activities for each student to complete before the end of the week. The student now selects the order in which he will engage in a given activity.   In addition, the teacher makes available more individual activities like puzzles, math games or equipment (such as cuisainaires rods or unifex cubes), phonics games, spelling games, etc.

These materials may be purchased or made by the teacher.   For example, if a behavioral objective is to help the children recognize pictures of different homes and decide who lives in them (social studies), the teacher might develop the following activity for individuals or pairs of children. On heavy poster paper mount pictures and/or illustrations of the homes in which people live.   Mount squares of felt beside each picture.   Paste felt on the back of pictures of people

who live in such homes.   Have the children place the picture
of the person beside the type of home in which he lives.

Or if one of the teacher's behavioral objectives for
the week is to help students become more proficient in rec-
ognizing the long vowel sound in words with a final e, she
might develop the following card game:

On 48 blank cards of playing-card size the teacher
writes 24 pairs of words; one of each pair has a final e,
one does not (rid, ride).   Pairs of words may be duplicated.
The cards are shuffled.   Each of four players is dealt 12
cards.   Each player tries to match pairs in his hand.   As
each pair is matched, it is read aloud and put face down on
the table (a book).   Each player then tries to make other
pairs by drawing a card from the player on his left.   Play
continues until someone uses all the cards in his hand.   The
player with the most "books" wins.

As before, introduce the activity period at the story
time.   Let the children choose the activity they want to do.
This can be done in the following manner.   The teacher may
say, "Today, I would like some of you to listen to a record

about a clown and draw a picture for me.   Who would like
to do this activity?   Timmy, Mary, Susan and David, come
over and start.   Who would like to work with the unifex
cubes?" and so on.   Each day the teacher should encourage
the children to do something different.   If they worked with
a learning game on Monday, encourage them to participate
in one of the group situations on Tuesday.

The Child's Checklist of Activity

One effective way of keeping track of what each child
has completed is to make a checklist based on each activity.
For teacher-planned activities which must be done at least
once a week, a simple one-column list of the class names
with a check space will be sufficient (see figure A below).
For games and general activities, a matrix list of class
names by the days of the week should be provided (see figure
B below).   It is left to the teacher's discretion to decide how

Figure A.   Figure B.

	M	T	W	Th	F
John					
Sally					
Jane					
Doug					
etc.					

Figure A:

John _____
Sally _____
Jane _____
Doug _____
etc. _____
_____
_____
_____

many times a week each student will be allowed to engage in
a given activity.   A chart should be available at each activity
and children should develop the habit of checking the chart
as they do the activity.

Some teachers find that jotting down on a file card
what each child has done each day helps them visualize each
child as an individual.   The children can help with this by
checking the charts or keeping a notebook in which they record their daily activities.   A combination of methods might
be used.

The Role of the Parents

Parents must be made aware of what is happening in
the classroom.   They, too, need to be introduced to the open
classroom concept slowly.   Often, laymen perceive the open
classroom as an unorganized play period--a free-for-all--
with little or no learning taking place.   Do not broadcast
initially the fact that the class is moving toward an open
classroom.   It is better to wait until you can let parents see
first-hand how their child is functioning in a more relaxed
environment; strong approval will usually then be forthcoming

A good means of initiating communication with parents
is to start sending home a classroom newsletter describing
the afternoon activity period.   Since the classroom is to include more active pupil participation, the newsletter should
be done by children or should include their work.   During
the fourth week of the activity period, the teacher can help
one group of children prepare a dittoed newsletter each day
to their parents.   A compiled letter can be sent home on
Friday (or on Monday of the following week).   Those children
with writing facility may do the entire newsletter.   If none

do, the teacher can write captions under pictures the children
have drawn.   The newsletter should contain descriptions written by the children of some of the activities.   The end of the
newsletter might include a note by the teacher encouraging
parents to watch for work that their children bring home from
the activity time.   The fact that the children are learning to
work well and think for themselves should be emphasized.
If parents express interest, they could be invited to come
to school to watch and help in the activity period.   In most
cases, however, neither the teacher nor the pupils are ready
for observers in the classroom at this point.

Chapter 4

SEVENTH THROUGH TENTH WEEKS

The next natural expansion in the transition program
is to extend the story-time and the activity period to include
the entire afternoon. However, it is of utmost importance
that the teacher feel comfortable with what has transpired
before taking this step. Likewise, the students (on the whole
must be able to work independently on a task that has been
assigned to them. Many classrooms should be ready for
this after the sixth week.

The Full Afternoon Activity Period

The expansion to the entire afternoon is a highly individual matter which depends entirely upon the personalities
of the people who make up the classroom. When they are
ready for an extended activity period, it will be easy to accomplish. In many instances, children will ask for more
time to complete what they are working on. Four basic
teacher-designed activities should still be sufficient for independent activity period and the teacher should be free during this time to do skill or review lessons in math or reading with children who need it. Also, independent activities
dealing with mathematics and language arts can be made
available for children to work on individually or in groups
during this time (see Appendix A for suggested activities).

In the beginning of the extended activity period, the teacher may find it beneficial to stop the children at the end of the first hour and redirect them to another activity. By this point the children should be able to choose their own activity, but they should still verbalize this choice to the teacher. This verbalization enables the child to think about his choice and to continue to develop this decision-making habit. At the same time it allows the teacher to check to make sure that each child is including a greater variety of choices. Some teachers like to use written contracts (see Appendix E). Knowing what is going on also helps build the teacher's self-confidence. Each child should keep a notebook in which he records what he does each afternoon. The teacher can then check the notebook at the end of each day and direct the child to include certain activities for the next day. The order in which the activities will be done should not be prescribed, and the child should not be prevented from making additional choices.

A Typical Afternoon Schedule

12:30-1:00 - Story time and discussion of afternoon's choice of activities.

1:00-1:50 - First activity period
If one objective for the week is to make the children aware of the basic skills of measurement, the following three group activities might be developed.

Group A: Works with the teacher for 20 minutes on the skill of using a ruler. Then they do seat work described for Group B.

Group B: Spends the first 20 minutes using a ruler to measure prescribed items in the room and represents them on paper. Then they work with the teacher on a skill lesson.

Group C: Works on tracing each other's bodies on a large
            sheet of brown wrapping paper. These will be
            colored and cut out. Then they will measure
            parts of the silhouettes with string and get a com
            parative measurement of height, arm length, etc.
            for various class members. The completion of
            this activity may take more than one day.

Group D: Listens to a skill tape developed by the teacher
            (or bought commercially), dealing with a phonics
            skill relevant to their needs at this particular
            time. For example, the objective might be to
            develop the ability to hear a distinction between
            the br and bl blend sounds at the beginning of
            words. A worksheet may also be developed to
            accompany this tape.

    Following is a list of individual and small group ac-
tivities which may be developed as additional choices (not
all in any one day). As always, the activities offered will
relate to the on-going curriculum and the objectives to be
achieved.

1. Groups of two to four children may be playing a phonics
    card game--which can be bought in any children's store
    or made by teacher or children (see Appendix C).

2. Individual or group of children may be working with
    unifex cubes.

3. An individual or a pair of children may be attempting
    to assemble a jigsaw puzzle.

4. Paint easels can be set up for one or more children.

5. Clay, with a specific recommendation for use (such as
    making animals for display), can be available for in-
    dividual or group use.

6. A selection of library books with appropriate reading
    levels can be available. (A rug makes a nice reading
    corner.)

7. A view master may be available in the science or so-
    cial studies corner with pictures of animals, customs

of various peoples or places to visit. (Again, related to the on-going curriculum & behavioral objectives.)

8. A balance scale can easily be made by teacher and children (see directions in Appendix C) and can be placed with a box of objects for comparing weights.

9. Magazines, scissors, paper and paste should be available for making books to support on-going learning.

10. A file box of dittos may be so arranged that students can be directed to it for review work as needed.

The activity period thus allows time for engaging in activities supportive of the morning curriculum, skill development, or interest development. A large selection of individual activities is desirable since children have a wide range of interests and needs. For children who might otherwise disrupt the classroom, it is important to have activities available which they can use successfully and enjoy. Even if, at first, a child selects to engage in the same activity for several days running, he should have the opportunity to do so until he feels able to move more freely among activities.

1:40 - The teacher should give the clean-up signal. As each child finishes putting away what he is doing he should be reminded to go to the rug and wait for the group. He might want to look at a book until everyone arrives. If the teacher can be free by 1:45 or shortly thereafter, this is a good time to sing songs, etc.

1:50-2:00 - This is a brief time in which to discuss what may be done during the rest of the activity period. The teacher should select a group of children to work with during the next activity session. The others are asked to choose their next activity, but again must verbalize their choice to the teacher.

2:00-2:50 - Second activity period.

If one of the teacher's weekly objectives is the
development of specific vocabulary, for example,
the following group activities might be used at
this time.

Group A: Works with the teacher for 20 minutes on develop
            ment of new vocabulary; then they do seat work
            as described below.

Group B: Uses specified vocabulary to write a story, or
            may be given an opportunity to write a story abou
            anything they wish. (At the beginning of the yea
            in early grades, this might be accomplished by
            the drawing of pictures or by speaking into a tape
            recorder. As students become able, however,
            they will do more and more independent writing.)

Groups C & D: Individual and small group activities. This
            includes some of the activities of first activity
            period, but with different students participating.
            An exception may be some child who started an
            activity which he wants to complete.

2:40 -   The teacher must be free at this time to initiate
            the clean-up for the day. It is important that
            the teacher help the children with the clean-up,
            but the teacher must not do it for them. Every
            student should be held accountable for his own
            clean-up at the end of the activity period. This
            is an important concept to introduce and under-
            score from the beginning.

2:50-3:00 - Discussion time. Teacher and children should
            discuss what was accomplished during the after-
            noon and make plans for the morrow. The
            teacher should be sure to praise when praise is
            due, both to individuals and to groups.

3:00 -   Dismissal
            The content of the afternoon's activities, as can
            be seen, can relate to language arts, social
            studies, science, skill reinforcement in mathe-
            matics, spelling, reading, art, music. The
            important thing is that students become independ
            ent learners--independent of the teacher, that
            is--for a good part of the time. They may wor
            individually, in small groups, or in pairs; they

may have choices of what to do first, etc.   But
all choices must be within the framework of the
environment set up by the teacher as a means of
meeting the school's objectives.

Communications with Parents and School Administration

Continuously throughout the transition from a traditional to an open classroom, parents and school administration should be kept aware of the progress students are making, and of the fact that the class is doing it in a relaxed
and stimulating environment.   A bi-weekly or monthly newsletter should be continued and sent home with the students.
The week that it is to be sent out, the teacher should allow
a group of children to prepare the newsletter as a substitute
for one of the skill instruction groups.   Many language arts
skills can be learned and reinforced while working with this
type of activity.

Another means of communicating with parents is
through the use of a polaroid camera.   Instead of working
with skill groups for one or two afternoons, the teacher can
devote the time to taking pictures of each student in the
class as he is engaged in some activity.   However, the
teacher should prepare the children for this in advance.
Most often the students will want to know how the camera
works, and a simple explanation can be made.   The students
should be told that the teacher is going to take pictures of
them as they work and that these pictures are a way of showing their parents what they do at school.   To promote good
subjects, tell them that their parents can see a picture of
them anytime and that this will be a special picture because
it will show them hard at work.   As each child's picture is
taken, he should be allowed to help time the print.   After it

is developed, the student should be given a colorful piece of
paper and instructed to write at the bottom what he was doing (if he can write; if not, he should dictate it to the teacher).   After the print is dry enough, it should be mounted and
pasted on the paper.   They should take the pictures home
the day they are taken, since their enthusiasm will be the
highest at this point.

Principals and other administrators are aware of the
trend toward open environments.   However, like many teachers and parents, they are often not ready for the amount of
activity that takes place in this type of classroom.   Keep the
principal informed of what is happening in your classroom.
Some of the following ideas might be useful for this purpose:

1. Send a child to the office when he does something very
    creative on his own.

2. Make sure that the principal receives a copy of the news
    letter which is to be sent home to parents.

3. Invite the principal to visit your room during the after-
    noon activity period.   (Usually a day in the middle of
    the week, after the children have settled into the week's
    routine, is the best time for this visit.)

4. If the teacher is required to hand in lesson plans for
    the week, concise detailed plans for the afternoon activi-
    ty period will convey to the administration that structure
    and planning are very much a part of the program which
    the teacher is trying to initiate.

5. The teacher should make certain that many examples of
    work that the children have completed during the activity
    period are on display in the room and at other areas of
    the school.   Most principals use a room's physical ap-
    pearance as a measure of the learning taking place in
    the room.

Project Work

The afternoon activity period is an advantageous time

to begin to orient the children to project work. After the
fifth or sixth week of the original schedule, they should be
ready for the idea of projects to be presented. As project
work begins, the mid-afternoon discussion group will usually
not be needed. The first classroom project themes should
be stimulating and exciting; at the same time, they should
deal with subjects familiar enough to the children so that
they can contribute their own ideas to the project. For example, a project around Indians can be a suitable spring-
board. It also allows the teacher to promote quiet work
habits since this is an Indian characteristic.

If the Indian unit is to be a good project, then every
area of the room, every subject, every person must become
involved. Most children will have some knowledge of Indian
customs and ways of life from television. Depending upon
the location of the community, some of the children may have
visited nearby Indian reservations. The children should be
allowed to bring as many items and contribute as many ideas
as possible to the project. Often, young boys have Indian
costumes at home and should certainly be allowed to wear
them to school. The girls may enjoy wearing long, colorful
skirts. The children should be encouraged to bring items of
Indian craft-work. The teacher, of course, should bring in
pictures, films, realia, construction materials, and books
to enrich the classroom environment. The teacher should
orient afternoon instruction groups to the project. This provides a good opportunity for the teacher to ascertain what
skills the pupils need in relation to what they are trying to
accomplish in their projects, and to direct skill instruction
to individuals as they need it.

The following list of activities gives an idea of what
might occur during this unit. The activities used should be

chosen in terms of behavioral objectives the teacher has for
the projects.   Four to five or eight to nine activities might
occur each day.   The important thing is that the children
become excited and involved.

1. Reading corner shelves should be filled with books on
    Indians.

2. A teepee of wood and burlap, large enough to contain
    at least two children, can be erected in the room (di-
    rections for construction are in Appendix C).

3. Indian sign writing can be introduced.   A book on this
    can be found in any local library.   Signs can be painted
    on the teepee and on murals around the room.

4. Indian skirts and jackets can be constructed from paper
    grocery bags (directions in Appendix C).   Children can
    also make headbands, etc.

5. Dolls can be dressed in Indian costumes.

6. A mural depicting what the white man learned from the
    Indians may be done.

7. Experiments with how the Indian used the wheel and
    cart to save him work can be conducted.

8. Experiments with shadows and sun and how to tell time
    in this manner can be conducted.

9. Indian tom-toms can be made (directions in Appendix
    C) and Indian chants learned.

10. The children can investigate what foods were most com-
    mon to the Indian's diet and then experiment with them.
    Corn, which was common, can be popped; or why not
    have the children shuck corn, boil it and then eat it on
    the cob?   A regular hot-plate can be used as the heat-
    ing source.   If a portable oven can be brought in, or
    if there is an oven in the school that can be used, corn
    bread can be baked.

11. If corn is shucked, make sure the shucks are used to
    make corn shuck dolls which served as toys for many
    Indian children (directions are in Appendix C).

12. A local scout troop may be willing to come in and perform some Indian dances for the class, or there may be members of the class who know how. The Physical Education teacher may be able to teach Indian games and dances to the class.

13. The students may make simple looms and learn to weave (directions in Appendix C).

14. Old beads collected from parents can provide the material for bead work.

15. Sand painting can be done (directions in Appendix C).

16. A group of children may enjoy making up a play about Indian life. The teepee can be used as the background.

17. A trading post can be set up. Here children can learn that some people use other things than money for exchange.

18. During this unit, the teacher should encourage the pupils to sit on the floor in circles and talk with each other.

Another, simpler project might be the study of the vegetable as a food. Books on vegetables can be made. Puppets representing vegetables can be constructed from paper bags and decorated. A puppet show telling the value of each vegetable can be presented. (This project can involve a visit to a supermarket to purchase vegetables. Parents can be helpful and participate in taking the group to the supermarket.) A good culmination for this project is to cook vegetable soup. Everyone should have a chance to help peel and pare the vegetables. Then everyone should have a chance to eat them!

These suggested activities are only two of many examples. The teacher of intermediate grades, which have social studies and science books, can capitalize on project work to make these texts come alive.

Activity Cards

Having the chance to contribute to the development
of a unit of study will help the children develop independence.
In order to cut down on verbal directions and direct supervision, the teacher may want to use activity cards to give her
children directions for activities during the afternoon--espe-
cially after they become involved in project work and the
teacher's time is needed to help those children who are
having individual problems.   The following are suggestions
to aid the teacher in the preparation of activity cards which
can be placed in appropriate areas to help children complete
or begin activities.

1.   The activity should be interesting to the children and
     appropriate for their age and skill levels.

2.   The activity should be stated in clear and simple terms
     --in language which is part of the children's working
     and reading vocabulary.

3.   All the steps necessary to complete the activity success-
     fully should be included.

4.   The children should possess the skills necessary to com-
     plete the activity.

5.   The activity should be related in some manner to other
     work in which children have been engaged.

6.   The activity should be one that can be completed in a
     reasonable length of time so that the student does not
     become bored.

7.   The activity should suggest future activities that the
     child might design and do on his own.

8.   The teacher should have an objective in mind before in-
     volving the children in the activity.

A group of books--Shape and Size, Pictorial Representation, I Do and I Understand, Computation and Structure,

and Mathematics Begins--has been published for the Nuffield
Foundation by John Wiley and Sons, Inc. of New York.
These make an excellent resource for activity card samples
for the classroom teacher's use.

Following are several examples of activities cards
which were designed and used by the author with children:

If the objective deals with telling time:

On a piece of paper draw 4 clock faces.   Make
sure all numerals are included.   Number each
clock and show the times:
1.   The time you go to bed
2.   The time you leave for school
3.   The time your favorite T.V. program comes
     on
4.   The time you eat lunch at school.

If the objective deals with understanding reasons for
measurement:

Cut a piece of string any length.   Take the length
of string and measure each of the following:
1.   your foot
2.   a window sill
3.   your friend's head
4.   the room's length
State each measurement in lengths of string.
Make a graph to show relationship of all four.
Tape your string on the graph.

If the objective deals with improvement of handwrit-
ing:

Pretend you are a moon person. You landed on
Earth in a rocket ship.   Leave notes for earth
people.   (Make sure they can read your writing.)

At this point activities and schedules should continue
unchanged until the children develop independence to work on
their own.   As this occurs, the children will need less and
less direction from the teacher.   When the teacher feels a
child is ready, the child may be allowed to proceed in his
work without verbalizing his intentions to the teacher.   The
teacher becomes increasingly aware of each student as an
individual and designs activities which help each child meet
the required behavioral objectives.   When children and teacher begin to feel comfortable in this setting, then much of
what is transpiring in the afternoons will start to carry over
into the mornings.   Children who are involved in projects
will want the chance to work on them when they complete
their other work in the morning.   If each individual child's
needs are being met in the afternoon sessions, then disciplin-
will be no problem.   Success will have been achieved when
children and teacher feel they can trust each other and are
enjoying what is occurring.   Reaching this classroom attitude
will require different lengths of time for different classes;
when it is attained, then the class is ready to move toward
an entirely open day.

Chapter 5

TRANSITION TO THE MORNING

Depending on the children's and the teacher's attitudes after having made a transition to an open afternoon activity period, some classes and teachers may find it necessary or wish to level off their efforts toward opening the classroom at this point. This does not mean that the teacher and children will make no further efforts to progress in this direction. The children themselves will be anxious to carry over some of their project work into the morning. As their ability to work independently increases, the teacher will find that she may introduce varied independent activities for groups not working directly with her during the mathematics and reading periods. The format for the morning's work may not change at all for these teachers and their classes. The change will be in the availability of independent activities to replace the traditional seatwork of dittos and workbooks, or at least to supplement and enrich the seatwork with independent activities and continuation of the projects begun in the afternoon.

The teacher may now set up one or two interest centers where children may engage in independent learning activities as an alternative to seatwork. An interest center is comprised of a variety of activities geared to the abilities of the learners and which extend or reinforce topics being studied within the classroom. The materials in the learning

41

centers help implement the behavioral objectives set up by the
teacher and curriculum. Each interest center and the materials therein must be adequately introduced to the children if
effective use of the materials is to occur without further
teacher guidance. The introduction may be by means of
large group demonstration, small group demonstration, individual instruction, peer teaching, paraprofessionals, parents, etc. The teacher may designate a corner of the room
for each center, or the materials may be placed on a shelf
where the child may go to select those appropriate to his activity and then take them to his seat.

For example, if one of the teacher's objectives is to
help the children develop skill in telling time, she may wish
to set up an interest center with some of the following activities:

1.   Make the Clock Tell the Correct Time

On a piece of poster paper mount several commercial
or teacher-made clock-faces with movable hands. Beside each face print questions or directions indicating
what time the clock-face is to show (for example, "What
time do we come to school?" or "Make the clock show
nine o'clock").

Make the Clock Tell the Correct Time

What time do you get up?

What time do we eat lunch?

11 o'clock

2.   Match the Time Game

Out of construction paper or poster paper the teacher
makes 10 cards, approximately 4 in. x 4 in., on which
she has drawn or pasted pictures depicting daily events
such as getting out of bed, eating lunch, etc.   Then 10
more cards are made on which are drawn corresponding
clock faces which indicate the appropriate times.   A
child or pair of children then match the cards.

3.   Construct a Clock-Face

The teacher places paper plates, crayons, construction
paper, and paper fasteners and a model in the center and
allows each child to construct a clock face with movable
hands with which to practice telling time.

Or, if one of the teacher's behavioral objectives is to
help the children become more proficient in distinguishing
vowel sounds, a language arts center can be set up containing some of the following activities:

1.   Make a Picture:

Materials: a manila folder
             a bright picture
             cardboard
             magic marker
             paste
             extra cardboard with words that don't fit the
                vowel patterns.   (It should also have a
                picture on the back and be cut so that it
                could fit the puzzle.)

Cut out a picture from a magazine, etc. Paste in on to tagboard or cardboard. On the back of the cardboard draw off six puzzle pieces that take up the entire back. Cut the picture apart. On the right inside fold of the manila folder, draw matching puzzle pieces. On the back of the picture puzzle pieces, write words that contain open vowel patterns for vowels y, e, o, a, i, u. On corresponding pieces drawn on manila folder, write the vowels a, e, i, o, u. Now add a few words that are not from the open vowel pattern and don't belong to the picture.

Make-a-picture activities are ingeniously designed to be self-corrective. After a child matches words and vowels he closes the folder and flips it over. Presto! Upon opening the booklet, a complete picture appears. Any error would manifest itself in a jumbled picture.

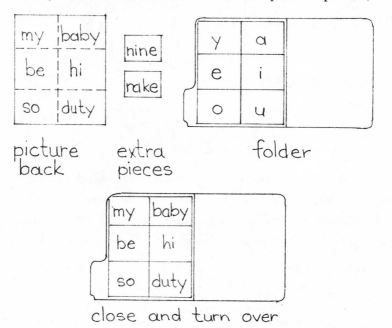

2. Spin-A-Block

    Materials: three 1/2-pt. milk cartons
                1 wooden dowel, 1/2-inch thick, 10 inches
                   long

2 thin wooden squares, 1 inch sq.
paper
magic marker
Elmer's glue

Directions for construction:

Take three 1/2-pt. milk cartons. Fold tops down to
make each into a block. Cover 4 sides (not bottom or
top) with paper. With the blocks side by side insert a
1/2-inch wooden dowel through the centers of the 3 cartons. Glue a small piece of wood on each end of the
dowel to keep it in place. On the four exposed sides of
the first carton print four consonants (ex. c, r, f, m).
On the second carton, print 4 vowels (ex. a, i, o, u);
and on the third, print four consonants (ex. n, t, d, g).
Make several. Place them in the language arts learning
center.

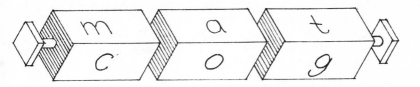

The child turns one block at a time until the letters on
top form a word. He writes down all the meaningful
words. The letters on the blocks can be changed to suit
the particular phonic elements being reinforced. For example, the middle block may have a vowel and r combination:

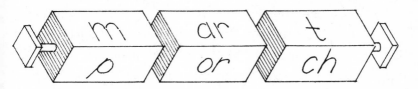

3. Double Vowel Rummy

Materials: blank cards the size of playing cards
a magic marker

No. of players: 2 or more

There should be a total of 84 cards in the deck when it
has been constructed. One letter or combination of double vowels, consonant blends or digraphs should be
printed on each card. Make 2 cards with each of the
following letters: b, c, d, f, g, h, j, k, l, m, n, p,
q, r, s, t, v, w (36 cards in all). Make 2 cards with
each of the following double vowels: ee, ea, ai, ay,
oa, ou, ow, oi, oy, aw, oo (22 cards in all). Twenty-
four of the cards should contain the following consonant
blends and digraphs, one card of each only: ch, sh, th,
wh, ph, gh, gn, ck, wr, sc, sl, bl, br, cl, cr, dr,
dw, fl, fr, gl, gr, tr, scr, thr. Two cards should
each contain an extra n.

The cards are shuffled. Each player is dealt 10 cards
face down. The remaining cards are placed in the center of the table, face down. One card is then turned
over. The first player may pick up the turned-over
card or may take one card from the center stack. He
then discards one card face up on the turned up card
pile. Each of the following players do likewise. The
first person to have a set of cards in his hand which
spells one word or more wins the game. All cards in
the hand must be used in a word or words.

Introducing Learning Centers

It is assumed that various learning centers will gradually appear to serve the afternoon activity period. Centers
are not introduced all at once or in a completely equipped
state. One does not go out and buy a center that is unpacked,
set up, and used happily forever after. Centers are growing
and changing things, reflecting at all times the objectives of
the ongoing curriculum. In the process of opening the classroom, the teacher will set up one center at a time. Materials will be put into a center gradually. Children must be
prepared for each new material so as to use it constructive-
ly. Special materials will be provided to serve the particular needs of individual groups. Some materials will be withdrawn when they are no longer functional, and others will

replace them.   In an art center, for example, only one me-
dium may be present at one time.   At another time, two or
three different media may be present.   These, in turn, may
then be withdrawn and other media made available.   In this
way the center remains fresh and challenging.   Some centers
will be phased out for a while and others set up.   The teacher should only have as many centers operational as can be
handled successfully by the members of the class.

Suggestions for the Content of Learning Centers

A Book Center

Physically, this should be a most appealing center:
a rug on the floor, rocking chairs, pictures on the walls
which relate to the books.   This center will contain books for
recreational reading, books to serve all the curricular areas,
and books which have been selected specifically to help children improve their reading skills.   Plays are particularly
valuable for group reading for pleasure and to improve fluency.   The following are very useful:

Houghton Mifflin produces a series of plays based
on folk tales: The Golden Goose and Other Plays, Reading
Level 2; The Straw Ox and Other Plays, Reading Level 3;
The Bag of Fire, Reading Level 4; The Crowded House,
Reading Level 5; They Helped Make America Great, Reading
Level 6.   Durrell and Crossley collected and edited Thirty
Plays for Classroom Reading, Reading Level 5, produced
by Plays, Inc., Boston.   Harcourt, Brace, Jovanovich, Inc.,
New York has produced a kit, The Story Plays, Self-direct-
ing Materials for Oral Reading, that would be most valuable
in the book center.   It contains forty story-plays, twenty
for boys, twenty for girls.   Each story-play has four

characters and four books are provided. The four parts
vary in reading level from 3.2 to 2.1 or below. The kit,
which is a natural as a means for children to help each other
in developing reading skills, sells for $60.00. Of course,
children should be encouraged to read to each other in pairs
or in small groups whether one can afford to buy these spe-
cially prepared commercial materials or not. Children like
folk tales, and The Economy Co. (Oklahoma City) has published two relatively inexpensive packets entitled Classroom
Library Packet, I and II.

A Writing Center

This center will provide stimulation for creative writing; music, pictures, foods and other objects to taste, smell,
feel, hear, touch, and describe. The opening sentence of a
story or poem can encourage a child to complete it on his
own.

Materials that can guide a child in the improvement
of the mechanics of writing will also be available. Specified
writing tasks with appropriate resources will be present as
needed.

A Viewing Center

Filmstrips, slides, cassette tapes, view-masters,
stereoscopic viewers, and occasionally, a film will be present here, with individual or small-group viewers. These
materials provide recreation or can supplement on-going curricular objectives. Visual materials can provide support for
literature and the social studies as well as art experiences.
This is one center where interaction does not depend on
reading. However, directions and materials can be available

whereby the children can also prepare their own visual pre-
sentations.

A Map and Globe Center

After some preparation, most children find maps and
globes fascinating.   Simple teacher-made or commercial
programs can guide children in a profitable interaction with
maps and globes.   Among commercially available materials
are:

1) Some very inexpensive booklets: Learning to Use a
   Map, and Learning to Use a Globe, published by A. J.
   Nystrom Co. , Chicago; Steps in Map Reading by
   Anderzhon, published by Rand McNally and Co. , Chicago; and Programmed Geography by Sullivan Asso-
   ciates, published by The Macmillan Co. , New York.
2) SRA Map and Globe Skills Kit, programmed for individualized use as are their Reading Kits; good but
   quite expensive.

A Listening Center

Records and tapes, with earphones available for a
small group, can provide a direct study situation, recreation,
and assist practice in reading.   As with the viewing center,
the listening center is a source of contact with other people
and their ideas through hearing rather than reading good stories, songs and folktales.   Many companies now publish books
with accompanying records.   The child can follow along the
printed page while listening to a good model of oral reading.
Bowman Early Childhood Series (Stanley Bowman Co. , Inc. ,
4 Broadway, Valhalla, N. Y.) is one; Scholastic Record and
Book Companion Series is another.   Others were developed

specifically to improve reading skills and aid backward read-
ers: Plays for Echo Reading, A Self-Directed Program to
Improve Reading at the Primary Level serves such a purpose.
It is published by Harcourt, Brace, and World, Inc., and
currently sells for $45.00.   Many of the Remedial Reading
Series now put out companion records.   Some are the Time
Machine Series (Field Educational Pub.); The Butternut Series
and Companion Records (Benefic Press); Dan Frontier Series
(Bowman Records, Glendale, Calif.).   Such materials can
serve well in the listening center.

An Art Center

Multiple materials in various media should be available in this center.   All children should have repeated opportunities to be creative in ways that do not require reading
and writing.   As each new material is introduced, some of
its possibilities should be presented to the children.   Some
children will require repeated exposure to a material before
they will be able to use it creatively.   Others will discover
a different way of using the material almost immediately.
Multiple easels should be available.

A Game Center

Table games, action games, and singing games should
be available in the center.   Again, all the games are not set
out simultaneously.   Games should appear at the table to
serve curricular and child needs.   Games will be needed to
review and practice language skills, to develop and enrich
basic concepts, to offer opportunities for repetition of basic
sentence patterns through singing games, as well for pure
pleasure and fellowship.   Games can be placed in the center

as needed by certain children for enjoyable drill in phonics,
mathematical facts, etc. Reading or mathematics games
may be placed in a reading center or mathematics center,
or they may be in the game center--whichever is more appealing to the children.

A Mathematics Center

Manipulative objects of all kinds for measuring, weighing, counting, etc. should be placed in the mathematics center. Measuring spoons, cups, pint and quart measures
should be available, as well as liquid or sand, etc. to measure. Rulers, yardsticks, and tapes should be there; items
to count or manipulate for adding, subtracting, multiplying,
and dividing; cuisinaire rods, cubes, materials for making
geoboards or geometric designs. There are some exciting
mirror books on the market for teaching mathematical concepts, and concept blocks are available commercially. Workbooks can be torn apart and sequenced for teaching skills.
Again, the mathematics center grows and changes to provide
the manipulative materials needed to support the current
mathematical concepts being learned.

A Science Center

This center should be set up to encourage children
to engage in manipulating and observing the world around
them. They should feed and care for an animal or plant and
observe its growth. They should conduct various experiments,
varying one condition at a time. They should use all their
senses as they taste, smell, feel and observe the items
placed in the center for this purpose. They should be encouraged to find the words to express what they observe and

experience. They should learn various ways of charting and
recording what they observe.

A Cooking Center

        This can provide a pleasurable activity for both girls
and boys. A couple of hot-plates are needed and children
have to learn how to use them without burning themselves.
It may be necessary to have an older child or an aide present. However, it provides an opportunity to practice reading, measuring, and following printed directions in a realistic, yet pleasurable setting. It encourages communication
and sharing. It can contribute to use of descriptive language
involving categories of color, size, shape, sound, texture,
smell, taste, touch. It can involve the emotions, contrasts
and comparisons. For kindergarten, this center should be
set up to resemble a kitchen.

A Sewing Center

        Sewing, weaving, knitting, embroidery, crocheting:
all these activities are of interest to boys as well as girls.
Each new skill must be introduced, and then materials provided for developing the skill. Older children in the school,
parents and paraprofessionals can be of help here. The center should be open to all children.

A Construction Center

        Children like nothing better than to saw, nail, build,
paint. Construction is possible from kindergarten on. Again,
children need to learn a respect for tools, for sharing, for
working together, for producing a good product.
        Construction activities can serve children's needs for

physical activity, for creative expression, and for serving all areas of the curriculum: art, social studies, reading and other language arts, mathematics, science. A puppet stage, a "TV box," a log cabin, etc. --things should be constructed that will serve the child, a group, or the classroom community. The construction activities will have to be introduced gradually and must be carefully supervised at first. As soon as children can read, written instructions for any construction should be provided, but should be carefully written so that the children can follow them successfully. Some construction, of course, will be purely creative. And at the early ages, tinkertoys, building blocks, pre-fabricated logs, and even puzzles can be considered construction.

A Dress-up Center

For kindergarteners or early in first grade, various clothes, hats, and shoes should be available for children to dress up in and act out a variety of roles. A door mirror should be provided. As social science units develop, the dress-up center could reflect this, with clothes and other props which enable children to play the roles of doctor, nurse, dentist, carpenter, plumber, railroad conductor, etc.

A Social Science Center

If such a center were set up, its contents could vary with each social science unit. However, such a center may not be needed at all. The whole room should reflect the social studies unit, and children can be directed to the viewing center, the book center, the construction center, where the materials would now reflect the needs of the ongoing social science unit. If Mexico were being studied, for example,

there would be a variety of maps of Mexico in the Map &
Globe Center, recipes and ingredients for making Mexican
foods in the Cooking Center, etc.

Those teachers who desire to level off at this point
should read the following section for ideas which they may
find can be implemented in their classroom without changing
the format of their morning any further.   Thus, during the
mathematics and reading periods, the teacher can simply
carry over into the morning the techniques introduced into
the afternoon, but with materials suited to the behavioral objectives of the morning's lessons.   Both children and teacher
should continue to grow toward more open attitudes and class
room practices.   The class will naturally continue the afternoon of project work and independent activity.

PART II

THE SECOND PHASE

Chapter 6

MOVING THE OPEN PROGRAM
INTO THE MORNING

After success has been achieved in the afternoon's activity period (when the teacher is convinced that her children are learning in a more relaxed atmosphere; when mutual trust has developed between the teacher and the children; when the teacher is able to view each child as an individual to a large extent; when the children involved are able to accept reasonable responsibility for their own learning; when parents have seen the results of learning taking place during the relaxed period of each day; and when the principal is convinced that the afternoon period is beneficial), then the teacher and the class are ready to venture into a full day of open environment.

As the teacher and children move beyond the first phase of transition to an open environment, a great many of the ideas being explored during the afternoon period creep into the class's morning. As the children begin to be able to work on their own, the teacher can allow a choice of activities after required work is finished. The trust, friendship, and respect for each other which was developing among class members and the teacher will certainly carry over into the morning. The teacher who meets success with positive reinforcement in the afternoon activity will likely use these same positive reinforcements in the morning, either consciously

57

or unconsciously. Consequently, the next phase of the transition to an open environment will not consist so much of creating new ideas as strengthening those ideas that have been formed and relaxing the schedule to allow for more individualization and freedom.

The Afternoon Before

Children who are enthused with working on projects and using materials available in the room will look forward to beginning some of these activities immediately upon their arrival at school in the morning. However, they should be prepared for the free part of the morning during the afternoon before; therefore, it is good to begin this schedule on a Tuesday or a Wednesday, rather than on a Monday. On the afternoon prior to beginning the new morning schedule, a long discussion session should be held. Here the teacher should compliment the children on how well they have learned to accept responsibility and initiate work, thereby reassuring them that they are ready for the next step. Tell them that the following morning they may come into the classroom at the beginning of school and begin an activity of their choice, or they may sit in small groups and talk quietly, but they must not disturb the activity of others. The teacher should also briefly go over the materials that children will have available to choose from in the morning. Each child should be encouraged to think about what he will do the next morning when he arrives at school.

If the classroom is to be truly open, the children must be made to realize that a quiet, orderly beginning to the day is their responsibility. The teacher helps the children by providing a limited number of choices at the beginning and helping each child successfully complete the activity he has chosen. Once the children have been shown how to do it, they must accept the responsibility for checking themselves in, negating the need for a roll call. (There are directions for making serviceable check-in posters in Appendix C.)

Arrival at School

The first day of the new morning schedule, the teacher should be at the door to greet each child on his arrival. For the teacher to bend over and whisper in each child's ear a greeting and a reminder to find something quietly to do can be a most effective aid for the children. The teacher should have placed around the room three or four games and independent activities. Also some materials and experiments can be placed in various science, social studies and independent areas around the room. These activities should vary daily or weekly. The teacher should allow children to participate in one of these activities or to finish some work begun the day before. No project should require more than thirty minutes. The teacher should also remind those who forgot to check themselves in to do so. After approximately twenty minutes, the teacher should give a signal directing the children to put away what they are doing and go to the rug area for a morning talk. While each child is putting his things away, the teacher can quickly mark the roll sheet from the children's check-in poster.

Morning Talk Session

The morning talk session following the short free-choice period is very important in the implementation of the next step, because it sets the tone for the entire morning.

The session should be warm and friendly.   The teacher
should take great care to compliment the children on their
entry and good use of free-choice time.   Their trust in each
other and in the teacher should be reinforced, stressing that
the success of the new day will depend on how well they
work and how well they can decide on what they need to do.
The teacher should explain to the children that there will be
times during the morning when certain groups of children
will be called to work with the teacher.   The other parts of
the morning's schedule should also be clarified.   On this
first morning the talk session will undoubtedly take more
time than the usually allotted ten or fifteen minutes.

Reading Instruction

Making sure that each child receives adequate instruc
tion in reading and mathematics skills will certainly be a
major concern to the teacher who is making a transition from
traditional to open teaching methods.   When beginning to open
the morning, provision still needs to be made for structured
group work.   Many teachers will need to retain some sem-
blance of a group structure for the entire year.   Others may
feel more comfortable earlier and will drop the group structure after two or three months.   The structured groups
should be kept as small as possible in order to provide as
much individual attention as possible.   For instance, if the
class is broken down into five groups for reading and five
groups for mathematics, these groups should be kept small
enough to teach a skill in about fifteen minutes.   This may
sound extremely brief, but if the children are concentrating
on what is being taught and are receiving individual attention
it is ample.   A follow-up assignment can be made for each

group. If a lesson occurs which will require more time, then one group can be skipped that day, with the skipped group being rotated through the week.

The teacher must realize that in the more individualized program of an open environment, reading aloud in a reading group may not always be needed. Time spent in a skill lesson such as reading should be a concentrated, invigorating learning experience. Let us reiterate here that instruction can be considered individualized even when a teacher is teaching a small group, if the group is small enough for the teacher to be aware of each child's errors and if follow-up work is provided each day to help each child overcome his errors. The teacher may also wish to listen to a child read on an individual basis occasionally; this may occur during the beginning period each morning or during the afternoon. One advantage to working in small groups rather than on an individual basis is that children can learn from each other in the group. Also, two or more children can be directed to continue working together after they leave the teacher.

Pittsburgh Case Study

In September of 1971, 30 children who had been in a traditional first grade in a Pittsburgh Public School were moved into a classroom which was to progress toward an open environment during the coming year. At the beginning of the second year, 27 per cent of the class was still at the beginning of the first grade reading program. Seventy-three per cent were at the end of the first grade reading program, but still in first grade reading books as classified by the Board of Public Education in Pittsburgh. Thus, one hundred per cent of the students in this second grade were below the appropriate level for beginning second grade.

This second grade class was first broken down into five reading groups and later into seven groups. Each group received 15 minutes of skill instruction at the beginning of the year with a 20-minute supervised reinforcement activity following. As the year progressed, the slower, less attentive students continued to have supervised reinforcement activity. Students who could accept more responsibility for their own learning received 15-minute skill lessons only, either in groups or as individuals. Later in the year, these more advanced students received formal instruction only when needed or requested.

At mid-year 27 per cent of the second graders were still in what was classified as a first grade book. Forty per cent were in the second grade reader but were one section below the level appropriate for this time of the year. Therefore, a total of 67 per cent were below the appropriate level for the middle of the year; the remaining 33 per cent of the children were on or above the level appropriate for this time of the year. By the end of the school year, in June of 1972, 30 per cent of the students were still below the appropriate level but all were well into second grade work; thirty-five percent were finishing up second grade work and thirty-five per cent were doing third grade work. Therefore, 70 per cent of the second-grade students were now on or above the appropriate level for the end of the school year as compared to none on level at the beginning of the year.

A Typical Schedule

A typical schedule for opening the morning environment might be as outlined below. (Note, during the first

few days, when longer periods of talk are needed, the group
work will be moved up and there will be little if any clean-
up time at the end of the morning.)

8:25-8:30   Teacher meets children at door of classroom

8:30-8:50   Time for individual work

8:50-9:00   Morning talk session

9:00-9:15   Teacher works with group 1 in reading
             Group five in math does independent exercise.
             Rest of class works on independent projects de-
                signed by the teacher to help achieve specific
                objectives which are part of her curriculum.
                These may include some of the following ac-
                tivities:
             1.   Using earphones or soft tape player
                  with syllabication exercise, if an objec-
                  tive is to develop skill in dividing words
                  into syllables.
             2.   Using potter's clay to mold something,
                  if an objective is to experience creative
                  production with clay as the medium.
             3.   Work on a series of drawings which will
                  be placed in a box to make a T.V.
                  show, if an objective is to develop se-
                  quence and story telling skills (direc-
                  tions in Appendix C).
             4.   Attempt a scale drawing of the class-
                  room, if measurement and proportion
                  skills are an objective.
             5.   Make a book complete with title and
                  pictures, if improving creative writing
                  ability is an objective.
             6.   Make up a sheet of mathematics prob-
                  lems to be done by a friend. These
                  problems should be like those being
                  worked on by the child to meet current
                  objectives.
             7.   Reading library books.
             8.   Doing a mural on animal life in the re-
                  gion, if an objective is to become aware
                  of local animals and their way of life.
             9.   Playing a bought game such as "Tuff"
                  to reinforce current math objectives.

10.   Using a typewriter (even a portable will do) to strengthen creative writing ability.

9:15-9:30   Teacher works with group 5 in math.
Group 1 in reading does independent exercise.
(Exercises completed may be placed in folders for checking later in day or week.)
Rest of class works on independent projects.

9:30-9:45   Teacher works with group 2 in reading.
Group 4 in math does independent exercise.
Rest of class works on independent projects.

9:45-10:00   Teacher works with group 4 in math.
Group 2 in reading does independent exercise.
Rest of class works on independent projects.

10:00-10:15   Teacher works with group 3 in reading.
Group 1 in math does independent exercise.
Rest of class works on independent projects.

10:15-10:30   Teacher works with group 1 in math.
Group 3 in reading does independent exercise.
Rest of class works on independent projects.

10:30-10:40   Everyone in class stops what he or she is doing and sits down for short discussion of how morning is progressing.

10:40-10:55   Teacher works with group 4 in reading.
Group 3 in math does independent exercise.
Rest of class works on independent projects.

10:55-11:10   Teacher works with group 3 in math.
Group 4 in reading does independent exercise.
Rest of class works on independent projects.

11:10-11:25   Teacher works with group 5 in reading.
Group 2 in math does independent exercise.
Rest of class does independent projects.

11:25-11:40   Teacher works with group 2 in math.
Group 5 in reading does independent project.
Rest of class does independent projects.

11:40-11:50   Time for teacher to catch up on anything not

done so far this morning or to work with individuals.

11:50-12:00   Clean-up time in preparation for lunch.   Room should be reasonably clean at this point so that children will be ready for the afternoon.

12:00-12:30   Lunch

12:30-1:00   Story time

1:00-2:40   Afternoon activity period
Children work on projects introduced and thought about in story time discussion.   Teacher may work with groups which need reinforcement from morning.

Schedule for the teacher may look as follows:

1:00-1:20   Help everyone get settled into work.

1:20-1:40   Work with group 1 in math for reinforcement.

1:40-1:50   Circulate around room to help those who need it.

1:50-2:10   Work with group 3 in reading for reinforcement.

2:10-2:20   Help group 1 in reading get on headphones or start tape recorder for recorded skill phonics lesson.   Help others who need help in room.

2:20-2:40   Work with group 5 in math for reinforcement.

2:30   Give 10-minute warning till clean-up.

2:40-2:50   Clean up

2:50-3:00   Discussion of day's activities.

Responsibility of Children

Children should play an important role in helping the teacher during this phase.   One way in which this can occur is for the teacher to utilize the child's help in getting together the reading group.   The teacher can rotate responsi-

bility for gathering the group.   Separate lists of the children
to be worked with each half hour should be prepared.   Five
minutes before the teacher is ready for them, the helper is
asked to collect those children.   A five-minute period will
be needed so that the children who are working on projects
will have time to put away their material before coming to
the group.   There should be space in the group areas for
those who might arrive a few minutes early.   Those children
who will be able to carry out this responsibility best should
be the ones to be utilized first.   This gives the teacher more
help as the new schedule is being adjusted to and provides
good models for other children whose turn will come later.

Discipline in classroom behavior is another area in
which children can and should assume maximum responsibility.
As soon as the morning venture gets under way, the teacher
should spend some time talking with the children about how
the classroom resembles a community.   From this discussion the teacher should lead into how communities are gov-
erned.   Even the youngest five-year-old can understand this
in simple terms.   For older children, a study of community
government might even be appropriate.   The children should
be led to think how they can govern their classroom and
what rules are necessary and why.   They should also be
given the opportunity to make these rules, determine the con-
sequences for breaking them, and determine how the rules
can be enforced.

A large group of 6- or 7-year-old children who were
participating in an open classroom experience in a Pittsburgh
public school was presented with this problem.   Until this
time the teachers had been using positive reinforcement in
the form of candy and a set of rules drawn up jointly by the
children and the teachers.   The children decided to elect a

group of representatives to draw up a set of rules and an
accompanying list of fines for breaking these rules. A mon-
etary system was introduced into the classroom community.
A large amount of money called "op cla" (taken from open
classroom) was printed on orange construction paper. On
Monday each child in the class was given 10 op cla. On
Friday of each week any op cla which had not been used as
payment for breaking rules could be spent by the child in a
special "op cla trading post" which included such things as
chances to bake cookies, go on trips, pop popcorn, etc. En-
forcement of the rules was left to the teachers and children
jointly. If a person ran out of op cla before the end of the
week, additional punishment was allocated by a representa-
tive group elected every two weeks. This additional punishment ranged from writing an I. O. U. for next week's op cla
to going to see the principal. The following were the fines
established by the class's representatives:

a. Fighting -- 10 op cla

b. Running -- 4 op cla

c. Making too much noise -- 2 op cla

d. Throwing food or walking with food -- 1 op cla (lunch
   was served in the classroom)

e. Throwing crayons -- 1 op cla

f. Keeping pencils -- 2 op cla (pencils were furnished
   by the school and were to be shared.)

g. Disturbing working people -- 4 op cla

h. Not coming to group -- 2 op cla

i. Pushing in line -- 1 op cla

j. Going to activity room without permission -- 2 op

cla (area for basketball, art, sand and water table etc.)

k. Taking things that don't belong to you -- 10 op cla

l. Crawling under tables -- 2 op cla

m. Not behaving in bathroom -- 3 op cla

n. Not checking in -- 1 op cla

o. Going in teacher's drawers -- 5 op cla

p. Eating candy or gum -- 1 op cla (a school policy)

q. Wasting materials -- 5 op cla

r. Bringing toys without asking -- 2 op cla

s. Breaking equipment -- 10 op cla plus pay for it

t. Not doing what teacher asked (if reasonable) -- 2 op cla

Room Arrangement

Even though open attitudes may be developing in the minds of teachers and children, the utilization of physical space to provide room for desired activities is also important.

New, modern furniture designed for open classroom environments is practical and useful but by no means necessary for a stimulating learning environment. Buying such furniture can unnecessarily increase the cost of an open classroom. The most important consideration is how to make the room arrangement attractive, relaxing, and functional. Rearrangement of existing furniture will occur naturally during the first afternoons of activity time and especially as children begin to work on projects. This entails no additional cost. Desks will be rearranged so that space is created for

each project area. As the whole day develops toward an
open environment, the arrangement of the room must also
develop to encompass those areas necessary for such an environment. Any classroom can be divided into areas simply
by moving desks around. The teacher should also remember
that once the whole day is being approached in an open manner, there will be no need for every child in the room to
have a desk of his own; more open space can be created,
therefore, if a few desks are moved out from the room.

The removal of individually assigned desks does not
mean that each child should not have a place to keep things
of his own. The personal space can easily be created by
asking each child to bring a box from home (shoe size or
larger); the box can be decorated and placed on a shelf or
stacked in a corner if shelves are not available. Regardless
of desks, each child should also have a "mail box" in which
papers that the teacher needs to check are to be placed.
The teacher can also use these mailboxes for notes to individual children; for example, the teacher can suggest activities for the child to do or it can be a personal way of giving

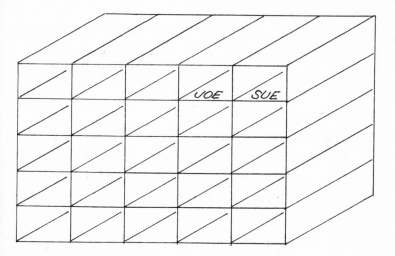

the child direction he might need.   These mailboxes can be
made from half-gallon milk cartons (with the tops removed
and stapled together).

Filing cabinets and storage boxes can be made from
cardboard boxes, painted or covered with self-adhesive paper.   Each child should have a folder in which to keep the
work he has finished until the teacher approves it, and a
folder for work which the teacher wants him to complete,
as well as suggestions for projects in which he might engage
These and the mailboxes can also act as low room-dividers
and noise-absorbers.

Each room should contain some place for the child to
be alone and or to work alone when he feels the need.   Study
carrels can be made simply by cutting the top, bottom and
one side out of a cardboard box and placing these on a desk
or table.   Again, these can be painted or covered to be
more attractive.   For small children, the space under a
teacher's desk can become a very private place, but only if
a child should choose it as such; it should not be used as a
punishment.   A tall appliance box with one side cut away,
the top flaps open, and a curtain hung over the open side
can become a "Be-by-myself corner" for anyone.   Children
need to have private space in an open environment; there
are times when each will need to deal with himself as well
as others.   Open means open with oneself as well as with
peers and teachers.

As individualization develops within the room, the
room will take on the characteristic of many areas devoted
to different activities--group and individual.   The teacher
can help her students develop interests in many academic
areas by making sure that all areas of the room are stimulating learning environments.   There should be: 1) an area

devoted to language arts skill instruction; 2) a comfortable
area for just reading; 3) an area for mathematics skill instruction; 4) an area for mathematics exploration; 5) an area
for science experiments; 6) an area for social exploration;
7) an area for art; 8) an area for thinking games and games
to improve perceptual motor coordination; 9) an area for
musical exploration; 10) an area for independent study; 11) an
area for woodworking; 12) an area for housekeeping (at least
through grade 3); 13) an area suitable for dramatic play;
14) an area for cooking in all grades; 15) plenty of open
space for project work, etc. A diagram of a typical classroom arranged in an open manner is included at the end of
this discussion; it should be regarded only as an example.
The classroom should be arranged so that the students and
teacher are happy and comfortable.

Much space is needed to store materials within the
reach of children. Shelves used as dividers between areas
can fulfill this requirement as well as help define areas physically and mentally for the children. Sources other than
commercial ones may prove more economical and feasible
for providing shelving for most classrooms. (A plea can
always be made to parents.) Often an old, unused bookcase,
lying around in someone's attic or basement, will be happily
donated. Some fathers may enjoy helping to make shelves
for the classroom. Encourage the children to be included
in this activity. Scrap lumber may be willingly donated by
a local lumber yard. The quality of wood and uniformity of
size are not as important as sturdy shelving. The children
will enjoy painting them.

Use of noise-absorbent materials will help keep noise
in the classroom at lower levels. Old rugs on the floor will
help control noise as well as provide comfortable places to

sit and read or to play games. Rugs which can be washed
simplify cleaning. Most parents will be agreeable about
donating old bath mats, throw rugs, etc. At least one large
area rug, such as suggested for the story-time area, will
add a lot of sound absorption capacity. Many rug firms will
donate or sell rug samples at a very modest price. These
make very nice individual seats and lend color to the room.
Hung on the wall, they absorb much sound and provide an
attractive background for pinning up children's work. (Hang-
ing is done simply, with two nails through the holes at the
top of each sample.) Lengths of colorful material draped on
the wall at varying intervals will also absorb sound as well
as providing additional space to hang children's work.

As has been said, one of the aims of the open classroom is to provide a varied and rich environment for the
students. Because of this, a variety of equipment is needed
which may not be found in a more conventional classroom.
Parents can help by donating things from the list below, and
thus reduce the initial cost of setting up an open classroom.

READING CORNER
Books of all kinds--picture, poetry, children's encyclope-
   dias
Cushions and mats for comfortable reading
Children's rocking chairs
Magazines--particularly children's or picture magazines
Posters, art reproductions, things for the walls

MATH/SCIENCE CORNER
Things to count (pop lids, beads, etc.)
Games with a counting or logic basis (spinner games,
   bingo, dice games, card games, etc.)
An adding machine (if available)
A Microscope (if available)
Things that measure (old baby scales, yard sticks, tape
   measures, meter sticks, measuring cups and spoons,
   thermometers, barometers, etc.)

Mechanical and electrical gadgets--broken small appliances
   to take apart
Shapes, colors, sizes

ARTS AND CRAFTS
Baby food jars with or without lids
3-lb. and smaller coffee cans (with or without lids)
Scraps of all sorts of materials
Paper, cardboard, wallpaper, etc.
Special adhesives (Elmer's glue, cement)
Fabric and felt scraps
Yarn and string leftovers
Styrofoam, tile, linoleum pieces
Ribbon, lace, rick-rack
Ink pads and printing sets
Knitting needles, crochet hooks
Needles and thread
Wood scraps, nails, screws
Tools that are still usable
Paint, shellac, big brushes
Boxes of all kinds
Beans and seeds
Jars, plastic containers with lids
Cork, wallboard, masonite
Aluminum pie pans and cake pans
Group easel (large strip of celotex, or corrigated card-
   board 2 1/2 feet by 8 or 9 or 10', on which one can
   thumb tack paper for painting or drawing, etc.
Sponges

TOYS
Tricycles
Buggies, wagons, and large-muscle toys
Games, puzzles
Air mattresses

MUSIC/DRAMA
Records of all types
Musical instruments
Empty TV cabinet
Puppets and marionettes
Costumes, costume jewelry, makeup, props, hats, badges,
   men's clothes for boys, etc.
Books or magazines with plays - enough copies for each
   of the characters

GENERAL FURNISHINGS
Floor coverings -- rugs
Cabinets, screens, clocks
Space dividers (old curtains; sheets of corrigated card-
    board which are available in large sheets and are stron
    enough to construct tables, dividers, etc.).
Large spools for tables
Large tubes or ice-cream containers for chairs (See your
    friendly hardware dealer).

Revision of Materials

The teacher who has reached this point in the transition from a traditional to an open environment may find a
need for the revision of materials to meet the increasingly
independent study demands of her students. This revision
may be very simple or complex. The first and perhaps
easiest phase may involve mathematics and language arts
workbooks already in use in the classroom. Depending upon
the worth of these workbooks, the teacher may decide to
present them to each child to progress through at his own
particular rate, with help as needed from his teacher or a
classmate. Some teachers may find that children will
benefit from rearrangement of concepts presented in the worl
book. This may be accomplished by tearing workbooks apart
and rearranging the pages. Other children may need additional
practice and reinforcement of certain concepts. The teacher
may accomplish this by clipping helpful teacher-made pages or
pages from other workbooks into appropriate sections.

Many spelling, health, social studies, and science
books will lend themselves to independent study. These will
be the books which present projects and questions for the
student's consideration at the end of each chapter. In con-
sultation with each child the teacher may select those

(cont'd. on page 78)

Bookcases provide storage space as well as providing space dividers. Low wooden, cork, or corrogated bulletin boards provide display space as well as acting as dividers.

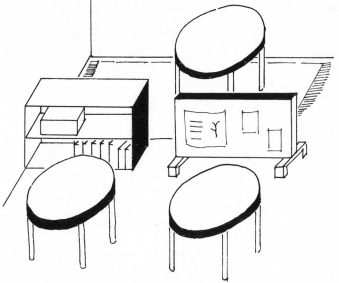

Tables and bookcases may be used to define a corner, such as a reading library. A piano may be placed in the center of the room rather than against a wall. The back can be covered with cloth. Thus, the piano not only helps define an area, but also serves as a display area.

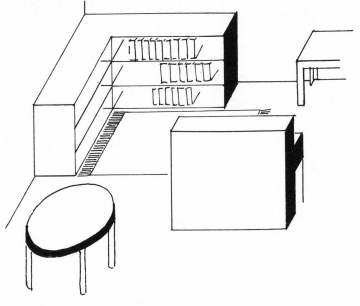

A rug placed in a corner becomes a place for teacher-led group discussions. Curtains at windows add cheerfulness and act as sound absorbers.

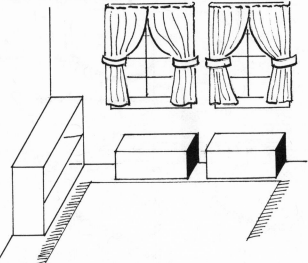

The arrangement of shelves and tables divide a reading area from an art area. The use of carpeting on a column helps absorb sound.

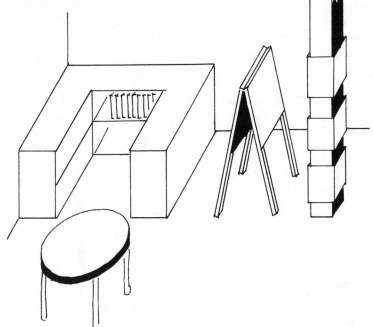

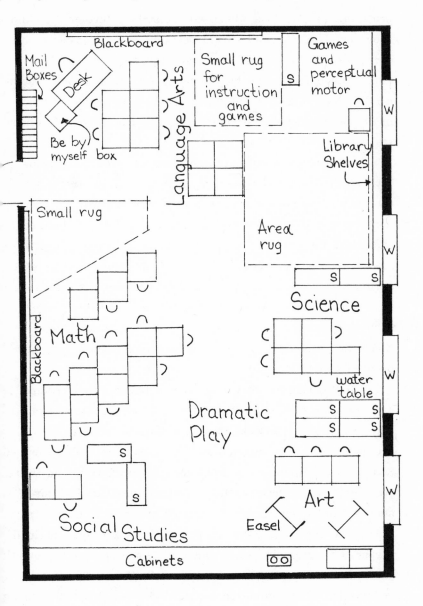

projects and questions which will most help further the child's
knowledge.   Each child should be allowed to progress at his
own rate.   When a child completes the text, the teacher,
along with other school faculty members, must decide whether the child should continue into the next recommended text
or if the teacher should supplement and enrich what has been
learned.

The teacher might utilize cassette tapes to help individual students progress through texts with suggested activities.   This method can be highly effective with spelling
instruction.   Tests to allow the child to check his knowledge
can be administered by tape or by other children.   Tapes
also can be effectively utilized in science; guidance for experiments, for example, can be recorded.   If a cassette
tape program is developed by the teacher, the tapes can be
filed in the order in which the students are to use them.
There are some commercial tapes available which may also
be used in this area.

Individualized programs in mathematics and reading
are available commercially.   SRA (Science Research Asso-
ciates) produces individualized programs in both of these
areas as well as in science and social studies.   Programmed
Reading is available on a developmental level from the Web-
ster Division of McGraw-Hill.   Programmed Reading for
students at the intermediate level or above is available from
Behavioral Research Laboratories.   These are systematically
arranged programs through which a child moves at his own
pace; there are self-test mechanisms built in.   The teacher
is provided with a guide book which will assist her in making
these programs an effective part of her classroom.   Many
of the new linguistic reading programs are carefully sequenced and come with supplementary readers that children

can read on their own. Some teachers will be fortunate
enough to have these available through resource libraries or
can get their schools to order them for them. Some of the
linguistic programs and their supplementary reading materials are listed in Appendix D.

Because the linguistic programs are carefully sequenced, teachers can easily assign supplementary reading,
workbooks, and games that children can work at individually,
in pairs, or in small groups. These supplementary materials will be reinforcing and provide practice toward developing fluency, yet all be within the phonics patterns introduced
by the teacher. These materials lend themselves easily to
use in learning centers. In addition, most modern reading
programs provide supplementary books and materials at the
independent reading level of the child. As with the linguistic
programs, these also can be used for pleasure reading, for
increasing fluency, or for reinforcement of skills currently
being learned. Children can read aloud to a partner or drill
each other on phonics, etc., as needed.

The teacher who has none of the above materials
available to her can still rearrange her materials so that
they function in a highly individualized program. Some
teachers put together "workbooks" for each child, using
pages from old workbooks as well as teacher-designed pages.
This can be highly effective but demands a great deal of pre-
preparation on the part of the teacher. Some teachers may
find it more feasible to prepare a notebook for each child
in which they list activities and projects in an order in which
they believe the child should complete them. This is similar
to a contract method of teaching. The teacher continues to
add to each individual's program as the year progresses,
always in keeping with the overall objectives of the school

system.   Ideas and hints as to progression of skills for
both of the above methods can be obtained from teacher's
manuals to any textbook series for all subject areas and from
the curriculum guides for the school system.

One other method can be of a great deal of assistance
to a more individualized instruction method.   In this method
the teacher prepares activity cards which encompass the
skills she wishes to teach in the order she desires, according to manuals for the subject area and the curricular objectives of the school system.   These are then filed in correct order and the student takes the cards one by one and
completes them.   Two duplicate sets of cards for both mathematics and reading (as well as any other desired subject)
can be sufficient for the entire class since students will be
at varying levels of performance.   None of the above suggested methods should exclude daily and/or weekly planning
conferences with each child.

Chapter 7

TOWARD TOTAL INDIVIDUALIZATION
AND OPENNESS

Scheduling--Teacher and Children Preparation

In most instances a class will be ready to drop the
10-minute reorganization period from 10:30 until 10:40 after
two or three weeks. Children will begin to resent this as
an interruption to what they are doing if it is continued for
too long. After this period is stopped, the children may
work in a free-flow fashion without being brought together for
total class discussion. However, the teacher should not hes-
itate, on days when the class is not working well, to stop
everyone and call a class meeting at any time of the day.

As soon as the teacher feels everyone is ready (whether after one week or one month), the day may be rearranged
so that skill groups can be called together for lessons at
varying periods throughout the morning and the afternoon,
giving the teacher a chance to work with individuals and
groups throughout the day. Groups of children who are
slower learners or who have shorter attention spans usually
do better if they have skill lessons early in the day. In the
public school in Pittsburgh, referred to earlier, there was
no noticeable difference in the learning rate of the average
and better-than-average students when they had skill lessons
in the morning or the afternoon.

Typical Teacher Schedule

A typical schedule for the teacher might be as follows (this includes only groups working with the teacher, not those children working independently):

8:25-8:30   Teacher meets children at the door.

8:30-8:50   Teacher circulates among individuals, helping and encouraging them.

8:50-9:00   Morning talk session.

9:00-9:30   Reading group one and mathematics group three each have a 15-minute skill lesson and follow-up work as in earlier schedule.

9:30-10:00   Teacher works with some individuals in science.

10:00-10:30 Reading group two and mathematics group one alternate 15-minute skill lesson and follow-up.

10:30-10:45 Teacher circulates around room, encouraging and helping individuals.

10:45-11:00 Teacher works with individual who needs special help in mathematics.

11:00-11:30 Reading group four and mathematics group two alternate 15-minute skill lesson and follow-up.

11:30-11:50 Teacher works with a group of children in the reading area, listening to individuals read.

11:50-12:00 Clean-up

12:00-12:30 Lunch

12:30-1:00   Story time

1:00-1:30   Mathematics group five and reading group three alternate 15-minute skill lesson and follow-up.

1:30-2:00   Teacher works with some children in art and helps an individual in reading. (20 minutes for first activity and 10 minutes with individual.)

2:00-2:30   Mathematics group four and reading group five
            alternate 15-minute skill lesson and follow-up.

2:30-2:40   Teacher circulates around room, encouraging
            children to wind up activities for day.

2:40-2:50   Clean up

2:50-3:00   Discussion of day's activities and planning for
            next day.

With this schedule, as with all schedules outlined in this
discussion of transition, time is only an arbitrary factor.
Keeping on an accurate time schedule should never take prec-
edence over responding to children's interests and needs.
What is not accomplished one day can be done another. Many
teachers may find it impossible at first to teach a 15-minute
skill lesson. In such cases, the teacher can assign an independent activity to the mathematics group one day and
work with a reading skill lesson for 30 minutes. Thus, a
skill lesson can be done every two days for each group. In
this enriched learning environment the children will still get
ample instruction and be able to meet curriculum requirements and objectives.

Gradually, as the teacher feels ready and the children
are ready, some skill groups can be discontinued and the
students from these groups can continue on an individual basis. Usually, the better students will be ready for this
first. In the beginning of this phase, the teacher may meet
with the skill group on Monday and make an assignment to
be done by Friday. On Tuesday, Wednesday, and Thursday,
the groups' time slots may be spent with the teacher working
with individuals or giving more time to some groups than
others. From this point, each teacher must develop a plan
for further individualization which is most suitable for herself and for the students. Some teachers will use a contract

method (see Appendix E); others will feel confident enough to direct each student individually in a personal manner. The slowest and most restless youngsters may not achieve this point of independence all year. They should not be expected to work independently without group skill lessons until they, as individuals, are ready for this. An open program which is concerned with meeting individual children's needs provides structure for those who need it. The teacher remains responsible for seeing that learning continues to take place and that the children meet the objectives prescribed for the school year.

Lesson Plans

Many school systems require the teacher to hand in a lesson plan for the week. Even if not required, lesson plans are essential if the teacher is to make sure learning does take place. After all, if children were capable of planning and executing their own learning, schools and teachers would not be necessary. Teachers who are not required to hand in lesson plans will be able to plan on a daily and weekly basis in their logs, as will be discussed later.

Most teachers, however, are likely to be required to hand in lesson plans. This not only insures that the teacher is doing adequate planning, it provides a model for substitute teachers to follow when they take over the classroom. Writing out individual plans for each child for every day of the week would consume far too much of the teacher's time and would be too difficult for a substitute to follow. Therefore, the teacher should plan objectively for small groups of children, realizing that time schedules may not be exact and that different methods may be used with different individuals to meet objectives.

Some principals require that teachers state objectives in the lesson plans. If not, the teacher should meet with the principal and discuss ideas and needs concerning lesson plans. One of the best selling ideas for objective lesson plans is that different children learn in different ways and the method of learning is not as important as the outcome of the learning situation. Objective lesson plans can also be more helpful for substitute teachers; any substitute should be capable of looking at an objective and devising some method of teaching that objective. The substitute then does not have to worry about finding specific materials listed by the teacher, if they have not been left out during the teacher's absence.

The following is an example of a portion of a daily lesson plan. At the top of the plan for the week should be a list of 10-20 activities for independent work for the week.

8:30-9:00   Beginning morning activities

9:00-10:00   Reading group 1: objective -- gain proficiency
              in distinguishing ending sound p̲.
              Math group 3: objective -- understand how
              fractions of 1/2 and 1/4 can be added and
              subtracted.
              Science lesson: objective -- understand prop-
              erties of articles which sink and float. .

10:00-11:00   Reading group 2: objective -- gain working
              knowledge of the following vocabulary: apart-
              ment, dweller, rusting, faucet, plumber.
              Math group 1: objective: understand what a
              fraction of 1/4 represents.

11:00-11:50   Reading group four: objective -- gain profi-
              ciency in use of pronouns which and who.
              Math group 2: objective -- gain proficiency in
              distinguishing between fraction 1/2 and 1/4.
              Reading group 5: objective: give individuals a
              chance to read to teacher aloud and alone.

11:50-12:00   Clean up

12:00-12:30   Lunch

12:30-1:00   Story time; discussion of afternoon.

1:00-2:00   Reading group 3: objective -- gain proficiency
              in replacing nouns with pronouns. ·
              Math group 5: objective -- gain understanding
              of what various fractions mean, i. e. 1/2,
              1/4, 3/4, 5/7, etc.
              Art Lesson: objective -- explore use of string
              and paint as art media.

2:00-2:40   Math group 4: objective -- gain proficiency in
              adding and subtracting fractions 1/2 and 1/4.
              Reading group 5: objective -- gain understanding
              of how to use when, where, and how.

2:40-2:50   Clean up

2:50-3:00   Preparation for going home and discussion of
              day's activities.

    For the benefit of a substitute, a list of each reading
and math group should be posted in the room, a list of which
groups will have art, social studies, etc. The teacher may
not follow these lists exactly, but they will be helpful to a
substitute.

Daily Log

    A teacher who is teaching in an open environment
must strive to be open as a person, to recognize and try to
understand her own emotions and feelings and the children's
individual needs. Writing down these feelings, emotions,
needs and reactions in a truthful way can help the teacher
develop open attitudes--this is a hard task for many adults.
A good method of accomplishing it is to purchase a note
book and to keep a daily log or diary. The teacher should

set aside 10 or 15 minutes of the day immediately following
the dismissal of the children as a time to write in the log,
skipping not a single day. Naturally, the teacher can not
relate in detail everything which occurred during the day, but
she should record the most significant items.   Among the
things that should be included in the log are plan evaluations
(how they were received by the children and in what ways
they could have planned better), notes on specific needs of
individual children (making use of error-analysis records),
personal reactions and emotions during the day (e.g., was
anger aroused unnecessarily?), and finally, notes on any un-
usual behavior on the part of any of the children during the
day.

The log need not be read by any other person.   It
serves its purpose if it helps the teacher to recognize truth-
fully and directly what is occurring in the classroom each
day.   As the teacher becomes more confident in an open
setting and more open-minded, it may no longer be necessary
to keep a log.   This is a highly individual matter.

Individualizing Instruction in the Open Classroom; Teaching Reading as an Example

Individualized reading has a special connotation in the
educational literature.   It refers to a child reading individually a book which he himself has selected.   Some of this kind
of reading may occur in an open classroom as supplementary
reading, but for skill building a different program is recommended.   The teacher must learn the skills of diagnosis and
prescription.   Skills will be taught in small groups; and, of
prime importance, each child must be placed in the group
most suited to meeting his needs.   If a child is receiving
instruction in reading in a book that is beyond his instruction-

al level, both he and the teacher are wasting their time and
effort. Nothing good is happening. If the pace at which new
words are being introduced is faster than the child can cope
with, he soon accumulates a backlog of failure which he can
not overcome. Then, the child and the teacher may begin t
believe that the child cannot learn to read. Therefore, it
is imperative that the child be in a group that is at his correct instructional level--that is, that he can master the new
material presented each day. This assumes, of course, tha
the teacher is keeping careful daily track of what a child is
or is not learning. An error analysis record is recommend
for this purpose.

Following is a sample of an error analysis record fo
one reading group. The teacher should keep such a weekly
record for each reading group.

Reading Group   Date:

	M	T	W	Th	F
Charles B.					
Mary J.					
Susan K.					
Joey T.					
Bobby S.					
Tommy K.					

Such an error analysis record may be kept on a 5 x
8 card, with the teacher recording during each reading session with a group. The record thus reveals clearly what
kinds of decoding difficulties each child is encountering. In

the light of each child's particular errors, the teacher is then
able to plan individualized follow-up by which he may overcome these errors.

For follow-up, the teacher may choose to work with
a child individually, may ask another child or an aide to do
so, or may direct the child to specific work in the reading
center. It may be that the child is moved to another group
where the learning pace is in keeping with his learning rate.
But in all instances, the teacher continues to keep an error
analysis record; it is the simplest means of remaining constantly alert to each child's learning progress.

An analysis of errors shows not only what a child's
decoding errors might be; it can also make the teacher aware
of problems in comprehension. For example, if a child is
asked to read "The cat is fat" and reads instead "The cat a
fat," he not only is confusing the structure words is and a,
but he is not making use of sentence structure. A verb is
needed in the sentence, "The cat is fat," and the child is not
making use of sentence sense if he substitutes an article in
that position. He has not learned to expect that each sentence he reads should make sense. Another example: the
sentence to be read is, "The boy saw a horse." The child
reads, "The boy saw a house." This is a simpler error.
Once the child's attention is called to the ou in house as
against an or in horse, he should be able to make the cor-
rection. However, suppose the sentence to be read is, "The
boy went into the house." Now, if the child reads "The boy
went into the horse," it becomes clear that he is not attend-
ing to the content of what he is reading.

This kind of analysis of errors can be made with any
reading program currently in use. There is an advantage to
using the newer linguistic readers, however, in that the

progression of decoding skills in more carefully programmed
and it is easier for the teacher to plan individualized follow
up.   For instance, if a child is missing such words as set,
pen, fence, step, it can quickly be seen that he is having
trouble with the short e and additional practice with short e
can be provided.   If the child is missing Mother, plays,
with, more practice with these words can, of course, be
provided, but all the child is then learning is these specific
words and not how to attack other words like them.   And if
his visual memory for words is not good, there are too many
different things going on in these words to explain them all:
m, th, er and irregular o in mother; pl blend, ay digraph,
and the inflectional ending s in plays; w, short i, and digraph
th in with.   This is so much for a child to grasp, and it can
occur very early in reading, in what might be considered a
simple sentence: "Mother plays with Jane."

Some of the linguistic reading programs are described
in the appendix.   They may be used as the instructional reading program for those children for whom a more structured
approach to reading seems necessary, or they might be used
as a well-programmed phonic supplement to any program currently in use in the classroom.   In either case, they can
assist in keeping a child's reading progress focussed.

Records of Child Progress

One item which concerns most teachers beginning an
open environment is how they are to keep track of each
child's progress without letting someone slip by without the
necessary skills.   A weekly error analysis record with systematic follow-up has been recommended for reading.   A
daily log or index cards on each child can help a teacher

keep track to some degree of individual progress in all
areas of the curriculum. Most teachers, however, feel
more comfortable with a more systematic method. A file
folder can be made up for each child. The teacher should
make up a skill checklist for each area of concern in the
classroom: mathematics, reading, language arts, spelling,
social studies, science, social skills, etc. On each checklist should be included those skills which children are expected to have upon entering the classroom and those they
are expected to complete during the year. Then, as each
child gains proficiency in a skill, the date on which each
advance was accomplished can be recorded next to that skill
in the child's folder. Not all children will learn skills in
the same order, and consecutive dates (in the order of the
checklist) should not be strived for. However, the record
enables the teacher or parent to see, at a moment's notice,
where the child needs special help.

Some school systems publish a list of skills or objectives that they expect the children to accomplish. Teacher
manuals for various subjects will also present lists of skills
which the children should acquire. The teacher should con-
sult both of these sources when compiling the folders for
her class. In addition, the open classroom teacher should
be concerned with the qualities of learning which an open
environment should promote in children. The following is
a checklist of skills in overall development that children in
an open classroom in a Pittsburgh Public school were expected to achieve. These children were in grades K-2.

OVERALL DEVELOPMENT -- OPEN CLASSROOM

___ To help child define his interest and develop the methods
to reach the goals he has set.

___ To work independently in a constructive manner.
___ To be sensitive to needs of peers.
___ To be responsible to provide for the needs of others.
___ To accept any designated responsibility and perform this responsibility capably.
___ To develop awareness of his own individual ability:
    ___ academically
    ___ socially
    ___ emotionally
___ To develop the ability to make a personal evaluation of strengths and weaknesses in performances:
    ___ academically
    ___ socially
    ___ emotionally
___ To initiate procedures of growth toward chosen goals:
    ___ academically
    ___ socially
    ___ emotionally
___ To be able to differentiate appropriate times and places for various behavior within the classroom.
___ To recognize the different expectations for performance in areas outside the classroom.
___ To develop the responsibility of behaving in an accepted manner while on a field trip with or without the teachers
___ To develop the ability to live and work cooperatively within a large community of children.
___ To be capable and able to responsibly:
    ___ self test
    ___ keep record of one's own progress
___ To be able to relate and respond to adults connected with the program.
___ To develop an uninhibited quality which will help establish a closer rapport with a group.
___ To establish a workable relationship with other children, both inside and outside the classroom.

Each child's folder, plus a parent conference not less than twice a year, can be a most productive means of reporting the child's progress. Verbal communication between parent and teacher can be a helpful addition to the open environment, a way in which each child as an individual can be discussed by teacher and parents. Not only do the parents learn more of what their child is doing at school, but the teacher can learn much that is valuable from the parents concerning the child and his reactions at home.

Many school systems have a report card which the teacher is required to use. The teacher should adapt the report to her own classroom environment as much as possible. Grades, it is hoped, will not have to be given, but if they are, the teacher should attempt to make parents and administration understand that the purpose is to show what an individual child is doing successfully. The teacher can also supplement the standard report with a written note to the parents--all teachers in an open environment will want to consider this approach, since a note can give the parents more insight into their child's progress than the standard report. The teacher should also use it as an opportunity to suggest things that the child might do at home in order to develop skill areas that are weak. In an open environment, homework should be done on an individual basis, and should be related to improving the child's skills as needed. The note home might suggest what the parent can do that might be helpful.

Most school administrators will not mind a teacher supplementing the regular school report if the teacher requests this before sending the supplement home. In some communities where it is hard to get parents to come to the school for conferences, a supplemental report can be particularly valuable in providing parents with an insight into their child's educational progress. Following is a sample of the supplementary report developed by the author for primary age (6-8) children in an open environment in a public school in Pittsburgh:

PRIMARY REPORT CARD SUPPLEMENT

ATTITUDES

RATING CODE: + = Satisfactory
                0 = Improving
                - = Not Trying to Improve

REPORT DATE

WORK HABITS			
Uses time constructively			
Takes care of materials			
Pays attention to task			
Follows through an activity			
Does neat work			
Works in an orderly manner			
Can carry out directions			
SOCIAL HABITS			
Works well with a group			
Is considerate of others			
Is friendly			
Takes turns			
Obeys rules			
Respects property of others			
Shows some leadership			
LEARNING ATTITUDES			
Shows enthusiasm for learning			
Has good degree of self-reliance			
Listens well			
Participates in group			
Takes pride in work			
Wants to help others understand what he knows			
Is confident in self			
Can direct self to task			
Makes good use of imagination			

ACADEMIC SKILLS CHECK LIST

LANGUAGE ARTS

Reads well in:

Comprehends what he is reading			
Follows written directions			
Attacks words independently			

Contributes to class			
Easily learns new words			
Relates sounds to letters in words			
Puts words into sentences			
Writes words with necessary neatness			
Writes sentences using new words			
Sees patterns in new words			
MATHEMATICS			
Recognizes numbers			
Understands number sequence			
Has adequate skill in telling time			
Has adequate skill in use of money			
Has adequate understanding of addition			
Has adequate understanding of subtraction			
Has adequate understanding of units of measurement			
Understands mathematical concepts of geometric shapes			
Is consistently careful in work			
SOCIAL STUDIES, SCIENCE, DRAMA, ART, MUSIC			
Has original ideas			
Is resourceful			
Shows degree of curiosity			
Works in each of the following areas an acceptable amount of time			
Art			
Music			
Social Studies			
Science			
Drama			
Comment on exceptional interest or ability in any area			
MOTOR COORDINATION			
Has good hand, eye coordination			
Has good control of large muscle movement			
Exerts reasonable amount of effort in games, motor skills, and sports			

Chapter 8

CLASSROOM HELPERS

Children as Helpers in the Classroom

A teacher cannot possibly work with 30 children at
the same time on an individual basis. As the classroom becomes more and more open, the teacher will find it beneficial to have helpers in the classroom who can do various
tasks and work with groups of students. Several possibilities
are available: the first is the children in the classroom
themselves. Tasks which might otherwise occupy as much
as 25-50 per cent of the teacher's time can be done by the
children. These include mixing paint (provide measuring cup
and spoons and recipe), putting up bulletin boards, passing
out papers, correcting papers (let each child do his own
against a master answer sheet provided by the teacher), and
making ready other supplies and materials.

The teacher can also have children within the room
work with one another. This includes slower students helping each other. Children can read to each other, drill each
other on phonics or mathematics facts, give each other spelling tests, etc. The possibilities for children helping and
working with each other in the classroom are extensive.

Children are often the best teachers of other children.
In individual interviews with 30 second-graders engaged in an
open environment program in a Pittsburgh public school,

twenty-six out of thirty children responded with names of peers when they were asked to "Name two people who help you to do your work when you don't know how." Only four children (the brightest in the class) responded that they went to the teacher for help. One basic concept of open education and of open thinking is to help the child recognize his responsibility to share his ability and talents with others. Children must also be taught to recognize their own ability and should have access to those who can best help them when they need it. When a child or a group of children is having trouble understanding a concept, another child who understands the concept might be assigned by the teacher to help. A child's explanation may make better contact with another child than the teacher's. One-to-one help between peers can be a most beneficial form of teaching in the open environment.

Older Children from within the School

Allowing older children from the school to become tutors for the younger children and aides to the teacher can be a most rewarding experience for both the teacher and the students involved. However, the teacher must be comfortable with the open environment and with the children before allowing others to come in to help.

Implementation of such an innovation must, of course, be discussed with the school principal and with any other teachers whose children would be involved. Tutoring by other children offers many advantages: the child being tutored may relate better to an older child than to the teacher; the tutored child benefits from the special time spent in such a one-to-one relationship and may also begin to regard

an older child as someone who can help him, and not just
someone who might bully him in the playground. The older
child who is to do the tutoring also benefits: he learns to
accept responsibility; to accept his more advanced knowledge
as an asset which can be shared with someone who is still
learning; and he reinforces the skills he has learned or is
still learning by teaching them to someone else.

There are several excellent sources of student tutors
in every school. The brighter upper-grade student can reinforce his knowledge and find a creative outlet for his extra
time in this manner. But the opportunity to tutor someone
else may also build self-confidence in a slower student and
enable him better to function to his fullest ability among his
peers. For the shy student, tutoring can help build self-
confidence which can assist him in being socially accepted
by his own classmates. One special education student assigned to tutor two first-grade boys had a reading level of
approximately 3.0 at the beginning of the year; by the end of
the year this girl was returning to the regular sixth grade
class for reading. A patient, understanding teacher con-
tributed a great deal to her new success, but so did the confidence she gained in teaching other children skills she had
just mastered.

The teacher should spend some time (perhaps after
school) with each tutor before assigning him a child or duties
in the classroom. However, what each tutor does depends
on the teacher and the needs of the classroom. Some tutors
will be used most effectively in working on a one-to-one basis with a child and reinforcing his reading and mathematics
skills; others may be used to work with small groups of
children in art and music, etc. ; still others might come in
to read in children and to listen to them read. The tutoring

can occur within the classroom and should occur during
school hours. Time should be arranged by each teacher,
but a 45-60 minute period is sufficient. For those tutoring
on a one-to-one basis, a corner, reading box, or nook of
some sort will add to the ability to concentrate. The teacher should outline what she wants the tutor to do in a meeting
prior to his coming into the classroom. While the tutor is
in the classroom the teacher should not interfere unless it
is absolutely necessary, so that the tutor's sense of responsibility and self-confidence will be developed.

The National Commission on Resources for Youth,
Inc. has developed some materials which will aid the teacher in working with tutors, and other materials to assist the
tutor in his work with the younger child. This information
may be obtained by writing or calling NCRY, 36 West 44th
St., New York, New York 10036 (Telephone: Area Code
212 - 682-3339). Books that have been prepared for the
tutor include You're the Tutor and Tutoring Tricks and Tips.

Students from Local Colleges and Universities

If the school is situated in a college community,
there is a rich source for classroom volunteers. The teacher may be able to arrange for student teachers to participate
in the open environment; but in addition to these, the teacher will find that students who are willing to volunteer one or
two hours a week on a regular basis will often bring many
new dimensions into the classroom. Such students may be
found by contacting heads of departments of education and
psychology. These department heads might welcome a chance
for their students to obtain this kind of practical experience.
Also, a call to the student center bulletin board may turn up

interested students. The students' backgrounds will determine
what they might be able to do in the classroom. Some may
want to tutor on an individual basis in mathematics or reading. Two industrial-design majors, who tutored in the program in Pittsburgh, spent their afternoons teaching boys how
to draw with perspective, design cars, etc. An art major
devoted her time to letting the youngsters experience many
art media with which the teacher was not familiar.

Parents

Interested and willing parents are an irreplaceable
source of help to the open classroom teacher. The wise
teacher will find one parent who is willing to be chairman
of the parent committee and who will undertake to find other
parents willing to commit a regular time each week as a
classroom volunteer. The chairman can also take care of
reminding each person of the need to show up at his or her
scheduled time. Many parents will be delighted to come into the classroom since this gives them the chance to become
directly involved with their child's schooling. However, the
teacher will want to feel secure in the environment before
talking with parents about this adventure. When the teacher
feels ready, a note home might ask parents to a meeting to
discuss the possibilities.

Some small group activities that the parent (both
mothers and fathers) can supervise or help with are the following:

supervising learning centers   crocheting
listening and reading to chil-   embroidering
    dren   woodworking
cooking   taking machines apart
knitting   constructing models
sewing   performing science experi-

ments	helping young children write
wood whittling	stories
pottery	helping children to work
clay	puzzles--simple to complex
painting	helping children with math-
weaving	ematics and other assign-
other art	ments

Another area in which parents can be of invaluable help is on field trips. The open environment should not be confined to the four classroom walls; if the open classroom is to prepare children to live in society and the community, it must extend itself into the community and into society as a whole. Field trips with large numbers of children and one teacher can be disastrous, and few if any children are likely to have a real learning experience. Willing parents can relate to small groups and thus break the large group up. Parents may also be willing to take small groups of three to five children on special trips to places that interest that group of children or serve a particular curricular need. Industries and even museums are much more willing for small groups of children to tour than large classes. Total class trips may be saved for such activities as a day in a park or on a farm where time is spent just enjoying each other and nature.

Professional Aides

Some classrooms may be fortunate enough to have a full- or part-time paraprofessional furnished by the school board. In many instances job descriptions and contracts will specify what these aides may do. The wise teacher will use the aide to work with small groups of children or in learning centers. Many of these paraprofessionals feel most comfortable in the areas of arts and crafts. Here they can greatly

enrich the learning environment.   The teacher should develop
a trusting, understanding rapport with her aide.   Both should
remember that they are employed to help children--not to
compete with each other.   The teacher should always empha-
size that whatever task the aide undertakes should be done
with children and not for children.

The paraprofessional can make many positive contribu-
tions to the classroom.   The aide may be able to communi-
cate with some children whom the teacher has difficulty in
reaching.   As another adult in the classroom, the aide can
help to humanize the learning community by giving individual
help to children as needed.   Very often, a child reaches a
stumbling block in his individual work and the learning process stops because he does not know how to proceed.   A paraprofessional can help a child over such obstacles and can
help each child keep moving successfully.   Like each person
present in the open classroom, the paraprofessional should
also be treated as an individual with individual rights and
worth.

A daily schedule for a paraprofessional in a classroom should be made by the teacher and paraprofessional
together.   It should reflect the objectives of the curriculum.
The following is offered as an example:

8:10- 8:25   Paraprofessional meets with teacher to discuss
              day's activities or helps to prepare materials.

8:25-8:30   Paraprofessional helps to greet children and
              direct individuals to specific activities or offer
              help.

8:50-9:00   Paraprofessional takes part in morning discus-
              sion.

9:00-9:30   Paraprofessional helps mathematics group with
              follow-up reinforcing group activity.

9:30-10:30   Paraprofessional supervises new art activity and provides motivation for children who are working here. This includes reminding and helping children clean-up.

10:30-11:15   Paraprofessional helps children working on language arts skills.

11:15-11:50   Paraprofessional helps children in science area with follow-up activities.

11:50-12:00   Paraprofessional helps and encourages clean-up.

12:00-12:30   Lunch

12:30-1:00   Paraprofessional readies materials for afternoon.

1:00-2:00   Paraprofessional repeats morning art project with new group of children.

2:00-2:40   Paraprofessional helps children working in mathematics center.

2:40-2:50   Paraprofessional helps with and encourages clean-up.

2:50-3:00   Paraprofessional takes part with children and teacher in discussion of day's activities.

3:00-3:15   Paraprofessional meets with teacher to discuss today's and/or tomorrow's activities.

At this point in time it should be noted that reduction of educational funds may make the paraprofessional a less likely source of classroom help. The teacher should therefore weigh carefully each of the other four sources of help previously discussed: the children in the classroom, older children from other classrooms within the school, students from local colleges and universities, and parents.

CONCLUSION

This discussion has been presented in the hope that the teacher who has been teaching in a traditional classroom will be able to make a smooth personal and professional transition to the open classroom environment. A structured schedule has been presented so that teachers may be more successful in their transition to an open environment. Once the teacher and the class have made a successful transition, the teacher will develop the structure which will most adequately support classroom activities and children's learning. The needs of the children and the means for gaining most active participation will be the principal guide to scheduling. The teacher may well find that planning for groups and individual follow-up is quite demanding. However, the teacher undoubtedly will find more satisfaction in teaching as a more enjoyable and successful learning environment emerges.

The teacher must remember that the children will also be making this transition. Hopefully, in the open learning environment, children will become more responsible, mature, creative individuals. Knocking walls out of buildings does not create open learning environments. Developing trust and good communication between adults and children and providing an appropriately stimulating and active learning environment does.

The ongoing curricular objectives will suggest many ideas for activities and projects. The suggestions for children which follow in the Appendices may be helpful.

APPENDICES

Appendix A

100 ACTIVITIES AND PROJECT SUGGESTIONS
FOR CHILDREN

1. Write a community story. Place as a mural on the wall.

2. Gather a group of poems. Make them into a notebook. Write your own poems.

3. Write books to become part of classroom library.

4. Publish a classroom newspaper. Use a typewriter, if possible.

5. Read with a friend.

6. Make your own dictionary with real or nonsense words.

7. Use a flannel board to tell a story to a friend.

8. Make a puppet stage. Make your own puppets and write your own production.

9. Practice your writing by using a crayon on an acetate pocket containing a writing sample from the teacher.

10. Make up a nonsense word and do an art project that describes it.

11. Blindfold a friend. Have him feel in a box and write a description of what he felt.

12. Label objects in the room with descriptive adjectives instead of nouns.

13. Turn the room or a portion of it into a zoo of words.

14.   Have a spelling computer--a cardboard box. Take
       turns being mister computer and answering your friends
       questions by writing on the paper the answer to how to
       spell a word, and passing it out of the box.

15.   Take turns one day a week and write something nice to
       put in each person's mailbox.

16.   Write books for younger children in the school to read.

17.   Made a letter file. Send letters to congressmen,
       teams, etc.

18.   Collect newspaper comic strips or pictures and make
       your own books.

19.   Write your own plays and present them.

20.   Write a book of favorite recipes. Try some in class.

21.   Read a book with a friend. Make a list of questions
       for your friend to answer. He will make one for you.

22.   Play Scrabble or Spill and Spell games.

23.   Play a phonics card game.

24.   Make a book of riddles.

25.   Pretend you are from another planet and leave mes-
       sages for earth people.

26.   Make creative pancakes and graph the amount of various
       ingredients used.

27.   Make creative pudding and graph the amount of various
       ingredients used.

28.   Invent your own system of measurement. Make a
       graph to compare items in the room which you meas-
       ured with your own system.

29.   Write a book of math problems for friends to do.

30.   Use dice to make up math problems. Throw, write
       the number down. Add a mathematical operations sign.
       Throw for another number. Complete operation.

31. Make a scale drawing of the room.

32. Make a map of your room, school, or playground.
    Take a walk and make a map.

33. Measure the play area.

34. Measure the distance friends can jump, etc.

35. Make play dough and graph ingredients you use.

36. Make a balance scale and make a graph showing com-
    parative weights of various objects.

37. Guess how many beans in a jar and then count them.

38. Use design blocks (by Milton Bradley) to create geo-
    metric designs.

39. Use string, nails and board to create geometric designs.

40. Use nails, board and rubber bands to make your own
    geoboards.

41. Use toothpicks and paste to build three-dimensional
    geometric designs.

42. Use large cardboard boxes and tape to create your own
    geo-design tunnels.

43. Practice math, spelling, etc. with a friend.

44. Bring an old adding machine to school and use it.

45. Play dominoes.

46. Design buildings, etc. using geometric shapes.

47. Set up your own trading post or store.

48. Use different types of scales to measure and compare
    objects.

49. Use unifex cubes.

50. Use Cuissenaire rods.

51.   Devise your own number stories from experience.

52.   Play chess.

53.   Devise your own calendars.

54.   Play 99 (card game).

55.   Play checkers.

56.   Play bingo.

57.   Set up a wood workshop in your room and use it.

58.   Set up a sand table in your room and use it.

59.   Set up a water table in your room and use it.

60.   Work with potter's clay.

61.   Make or buy a loom and learn to weave.

62.   Learn to knit.

63.   Learn to crochet.

64.   See if someone will lend your room a sewing machine and help you and your classmates learn to sew.

65.   Find an old tumbling mat for tumbling in the room.

66.   Make a model house.

67.   Design clothes and make a dress for yourself or a doll.

68.   Use dress patterns.

69.   Invent a country and make a map. Write about the country, draw pictures of its people, etc.

70.   Bring animals to class--hamster, rabbits, snakes, etc.

71.   Have fish in your classroom and take care of them.

72.   Hatch tadpoles.

73.   Hatch chicken eggs.

74. Use a microscope or magnifying glass to look at hair, salt, string, skin, blood, water, etc.

75. Learn to macramé.

76. Make curtains for the classroom's windows.

77. Make your own board games and teach the rules to friends.

78. Play Monopoly.

79. Play concentration.

80. Make your own tapes of stories, games, outdoor sounds, etc.

81. Make your own filmstrips (material can be ordered from Appel-Media).

82. Use a video-taping machine for your own productions.

83. Make transparencies.

84. Make relief maps.

85. Make a volcano that goes off.

86. Have a garden outdoors or in flower boxes inside.

87. Take apart worn out machines.

88. Make simple machines from blocks, pulley, rope, etc.

89. Make constellation patterns from a cardboard box painted black with holes punched in the top for constellation patterns.

90. Draw an outline of your body and place organs on it.

91. Cut out pictures of famous people, paste on cardboard and cut apart to make puzzles.

92. Make a card game of community helpers.

93. Use foreign language records. Listen to story and song records.

94. Make your own musical instruments and compose your own music.

95. Use your body in response to music.

96. Make books on various countries.

97. Cook foods from other lands.

98. Line a box with white paper for viewing filmstrips. Project filmstrips on it.

99. Be on a team in charge of a daily or weekly newscast.

100. Have an "Everyone-Read-Time"--include the teacher.

Appendix B

101 WAYS TO MAKE BOOKS POPULAR

PROFESSIONAL RESPONSIBILITIES

1. Read!
2. Talk about your reading experiences.
3. Send a book to another teacher (by your least interested youngster).
4. For one reading period regularly join your children as you each independently enjoy a favorite book. Read with them at your level.
5. Keep up with the best new juvenile books.
6. Attend professional meetings and read professional journals.
7. Talk to colleagues about good children's books.

SURROUND CHILDREN WITH GOOD BOOKS

1. Have paperbacks in your room.
2. Bring library books by the armload on a regular basis, choosing several for each child specifically.
3. Have children make book jackets for room books they have read. Permanency may be attained with clear contact paper--semi-permanency with saran wrap.
4. Have a file in your room of comments by children about books they have read and liked.
5. Have a simple check-out system. The child signs his name on the book card and puts it in the library box set up for that purpose. When he returns the book, he crosses out his name, and replaces the card in the book pocket.
6. Set aside a time for book auctions weekly.
7. Use prize money to buy carefully selected additions to your class's library--make a learning experience out of the selection.

8.   Take the book selection committee (don't be above "fix-
     ing" the committee to include children who need stimu-
     lating) to a bookstore to buy the room's new books.

PHYSICAL SETTING

1.   Have a reading corner.
2.   Create a place where reading is comfortable--an easy
     chair or rocker or a big floor pillow. Place carpeting
     pieces for "floor sitting" reading.
3.   Use book covers--real and pupil made--to create a
     colorful interest area.
4.   Have the materials present for the children to make
     their own books. Take apart old textbooks, and let the
     children make individual books out of some of the selec-
     tions. Each child can design his own cover for his se-
     lection.

Bulletin Boards

5.   Make a Book Worm: Each child adds a segment con-
     taining the name of a book he read to make it grow.
     Thumb-nail sketches can also be written on the seg-
     ments.
6.   Make a book tree, with each leaf bearing the name or
     review of a book.
7.   Stretch a cord across the bulletin board--or across the
     room. With clothes pins, fasten paper cutouts of book
     jackets or reviews of books. Entitle it "A Line of
     Good Books."
8.   Have children decorate a bulletin board with pictures of
     people laughing, surrounded by incidents from funny
     stories.
9.   Make a mystery, folk tale, ghost story, or other spe-
     cial bulletin board. Change the subject regularly.

CREATIVE ACTIVITIES ᴿ᛬ THE CHILDREN

1.   Encourage children to construct a miniature stage-set-
     ting for a scene from a favorite book, play or poem.
     (A box laid on its side is ideal.)
2.   A class- or student-made poster for the reading corner
     or the front hall may encourage general reading or
     "sell" one book.
3.   Encourage children to create original illustrations for a

selection.   They could provide a "series."   These can
then be put up on a bulletin board, along the blackboard,
or presented on the "TV box."

4. A picture postcard to each child's home from a trip or
    during a holiday period stirs interest.
5. Charades or pantomimes of books whet the appetite of
    other children while providing a creative experience for
    the actors.
6. Especially artistic children can give a chalk talk about
    favorite literature.
7. Class murals beat mimeographed bunnies and silhouettes
    of George and Abe.   White or plain colored shelf paper
    not "de-bugged" is inexpensive.
8. Book marks make practical creative work and might be
    appropriate gifts.
9. Letters or stories written from the point of view of the
    story characters provide opportunities for creative writ-
    ing as well as creative thinking.
10. Coathangers are easy foundations for mobiles.
11. Writing their own books in their words, by dictation for
    beginning readers, is valuable for all age and ability
    levels.
12. Making books--sewing and binding them with illustrated
    covers--encourages enjoyment of all books.

PARENTAL INVOLVEMENT

1. Encourage parents to read by offering books of interest
    to them as well as your paperback list for children.
2. Have PTA meetings about books, the library, etc.
3. Discuss children's book favorites during parent confer-
    ences.
4. Organize a book discussion group including parents,
    teachers and pupils.
5. Get parents to act as volunteers in your library or
    paperback bookstore.   Get parents to take small groups
    of children to the neighborhood library.
6. Particularly interested parents might agree to supply
    a story-telling service.   Provide training in oral
    presentation and use their services before school, dur-
    ing rainy day lunch periods, for released time for staff
    development.

TEACHING STRATEGIES

1. Set up situations encouraging children to use information

from books read to actually do something--a collection, a terrarium, an exhibit, a science experiment, a map presentation, etc.

2. Time lines, colorful and pictorial, can be a natural outgrowth of historical books. A class project might result from several children reading different historical novels of New England (Johnny Tremain, Carry on Mr. Bowditch, The Witch of Blackbird Pond).

3. Take advantage of the school public address system to encourage an enjoyment of literature--presentation of a special poem or limerick.

4. Story-telling or reading by older children to lower grade classes is to everyone's advantage.

5. The year they are too old to wear costumes at Hallowe'en, ease them through the transition with a special day to dress as a book character.

6. Have most advanced children compare Nancy Drew and the Hardy Boys with Treasure Island or another good mystery. See if you can help them read and think more critically.

7. Give an open-ended interest inventory to find out the kinds of books each child likes and why.

8. Chinese reading of literature at their independent reading level by primary-grade youngsters is effective and need not be noisy.

LIBRARY

1. Go with your children.

2. Go on the weekend to the public library and tell the class about it.

3. Review the use of the library so children can be comfortable with its services.

4. Let your children share the joy of using the Children's Catalog (or other source) to select room library books.

5. Involve children in book selection by letting them review new books.

6. Find some space to make a primary library. Have shelves coded by reading level so you can direct children to books they can read.

7. Use students to do clerical library procedures.

8. Encourage appropriate library behavior by positive rather than negative approaches.

9. Know your public library program, story-telling schedule, etc.

10. Meet your librarians. (Do nice things for them--you need their help.)

11. Encourage allowing your school library to be available before and after school, Saturdays and summers.
12. An oral library of tapes can be built up by cooperating teachers for children to listen to as they silently follow the words of the book. This is particularly valuable to non-English speaking children and for children whose parents do not read to them at home.

PRESENTING LITERATURE ORALLY

1. Choose some books they cannot read--and some they have. Regularly check to be sure that a variety of subjects and literary style are being offered.
2. Time is so precious--use only the best, yet appealing books.
3. Read often and regularly--not as a reward or spare-time filler.
4. Occasionally, have a story told to musical accompaniment.
5. Make use of films, records, filmstrips.
6. Tape stories yourself for a listening station--let children prepare stories on tape.
7. Encourage good oral readers to present passages, poems or short stories to the class.

Perfecting your technique

8. Rehearse your story orally, if possible.
9. Speak slowly and clearly.
10. Reduce the rate drastically when reading poetry.
11. Prepare the story for those who have and for those who have not heard it.
12. Anticipate words or concepts that need explanation to avoid interruption of the presentation by you or your class.

REPORTING ON BOOKS

One of the best sources for book reporting is Easy in English by Mauree Applegate (Harper and Row, 1963). For informal reporting let each child use the first and any other two of the following:

1. Name the author of the book giving the reason for liking or not liking it.

2. Tell what a favorite character was like. (Let the student draw or show a picture if he likes.)
3. Tell the most interesting part of the book.
4. Tell the whole story in a few words. (This item is dynamite. There is no such thing as a few words when children are telling about a favorite book.)
5. Read an interesting excerpt from the book.
6. Let children teach the class three of the most interesting words a book used.
7. Ask children to tell what they have found out about the author of the book, telling what other books of his they have read.

Creative book reports--written

8. Before reading a book with an intriguing title, encourage children to write down what they expect the story to be like.
9. Write an interview
   a) between a character in the book and the author
   b) between reader and the author
   c) between two characters in the book
   d) between reader and friend about the book.

Suggest that pupils:

10. Write an entirely different ending to the story.
11. Write another episode as an added small chapter.
12. Write a letter of appreciation to an admired author asking him questions and sharing their thoughts.
13. Write a book report in verse.
14. Pretend to visit the person whose biography has been read.
15. Write a book column for the school or class paper, changing columnists often.

Oral reports that are different

16. Each of four or five persons read a different book by the same author; then arrange a panel discussion covering such questions as: How are these books alike? How different? What are this author's greatest strengths? Weaknesses? How did you feel about this author from reading one book? (Each panelist should sketch or outline his story briefly before the actual discussion.)

17. Arrange book reports as a television program. ("I
     Have a Secret," for instance.)
18. Have students pretend to be a favorite reporter on
     radio or TV, reporting on a book in such a way that
     listeners will want to read the book.
19. Pupils might choose a lively scene from a book and
     either dramatize or make a puppet play of it.
20. Have one child interview another, pretending to be the
     author of a book both have read.
21. Have children prepare a hand-rolled movie of a book
     read.
22. Pupils may make a radio or TV play on a favorite
     book; recording it, presenting it to another grade, or
     presenting it over the public address system. (Reluc-
     tant older readers enjoy this preparation of Caldecott
     books for younger children.)
23. Have students pretend to be a book--advertise what is
     between the pages.
24. Allow the class to get together some favorite children's
     books from their grandmother's day. Analyze the dif-
     ference. Invite a few "grandmothers" in to tell about
     their literature.
25. Perhaps a few especially creative children would like
     to pretend to be their own children and compare their
     own books of the year 2000 with the books of the older
     generation in the late 1900's. (This is real fun for
     gifted children.)
26. Have a school party to which every one comes as a
     book character. Plan a program with a few prizes.
27. Make use of the overhead projector to allow children
     to give multi-media reviews to the class. Plastic of
     many varieties can be utilized for the transparencies.

Appendix C

DIRECTIONS FOR SUGGESTED ACTIVITIES

PHONICS CARD GAME:

Take 3 x 5 cards. Paste or draw a picture representing a beginning sound (or ending, blends, diphthongs, etc.
on each card. At least 48 cards should make up a set.
Rules for the game are similar to old maid. Two or four
players may play. The cards are dealt out among the players. Each player then takes a turn drawing from another
player. The objective is to make as many books of beginning sounds, etc. as possible. The child must name the
picture containing that sound in the correct position. Twelve
beginning sounds occur in the game; four cards should be
present for each sound. Thus a book will consist of four
cards. The pictures and sounds to be represented are selected in terms of the particular practice the children need
in a skill at that time.

BALANCE SCALE:

Objective: Construct a balance scale on which objects
of various sizes and weights can be weighed relative to each
other.

Materials: Block of wood at least 12'' square; block
of wood 2 x 2 x 12 approximately; three 10-penny nails; one
standard wooden foot ruler; string; and two aluminum foil

pans (the type used to package individual frozen pies).

Directions: Assemble the materials as shown in the following diagram. The pie pans serve as weighing platforms; the holes are punched in the ruler at the 1 1/2", 6", and 10 1/2" marks.

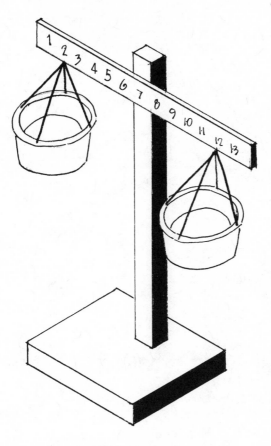

CLASSROOM TEEPEE:

Objective: Construct a teepee sufficiently large to allow the entrance of 3 or 4 children simultaneously. To be used as the focal point of classroom Indian studies.

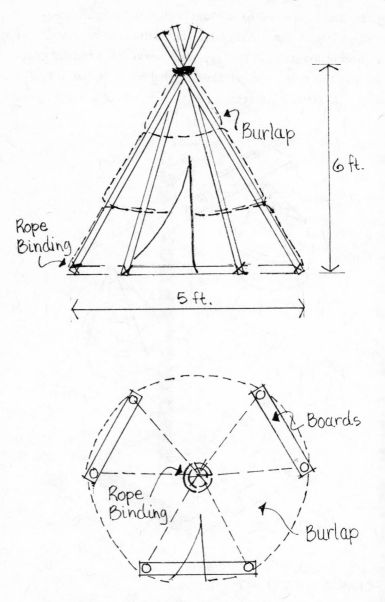

Materials: six 7 1/2-foot light-weight wooden poles
(bamboo, small trees, etc.); 50 feet of rope; three 2 x 4's
cut 3 feet 6 inches long; 12 yards of burlap.

Directions: Attach with nails the bottom end of two poles to the ends of each 2 x 4 strip. Bind together with rope the tops of the poles of each section. Next, lay the boards (with poles laying out) in the circular position as shown in the plans. Using more rope, tie each pole to the other in a clockwise direction. Next, tilt the pairs of tops of poles together, two at a time, and bind with the remaining rope. Starting at the top, lay the burlap around the poles and staple to secure. Finally cut a flap in one section of the side to allow entrance.

INDIAN JACKETS:

Materials needed: large grocery bags and scissors

Directions: Take grocery bag in folded position. Make one cut for the neck and the arms will be cut also. (No side cut is needed due to the fold in the bag. Arm holes will be made if the teacher cuts the neck hole wide enough. The arm holes may need to be enlarged or cut if they don't come out correctly.) Slit the front middle. Fringe the bottom. Use crayons to decorate.

Fold in bag ⟶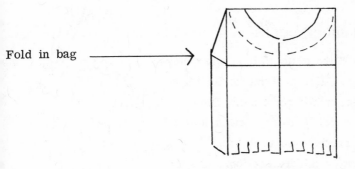

INDIAN SKIRTS:

Brown wrapping paper may be cut to fit around the waist. It can be fastened with a safety pin. Fringe the bottom and decorate with crayons.

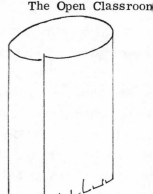

INDIAN TOM TOMS:

Materials needed: coffee cans with both ends out; oil cloth; heavy string or twine.

Directions: Cut the oil cloth into circles one inch larger than the end of the can. Punch holes 1/2 inch from the edge of the oil cloth circle. With the string, lace the two

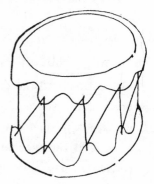

circles of oil cloth together so that one is on each end of the can.

CORN SHUCK DOLLS:

Take a fist full of the shucks of corn. Use a string to tie off a top section for the head. Divide the remaining lower portion into 2 small sections on each side and one larger middle section. Tie the small sections off and trim about 2 or 3 inches. This will be the

arms.   Decorate trunk and face with buttons stuck on with short pins.

CARDBOARD LOOMS:

Take a rectangular piece of cardboard.   Cut slits on each end exactly the same distance apart.   Take yarn and hook one piece across the cardboard with its ends securely fastened in the two opposing slits.   Repeat for each pair of slits in the cardboard.   Now take a long length of yarn and weave in and out of the cross yarn.

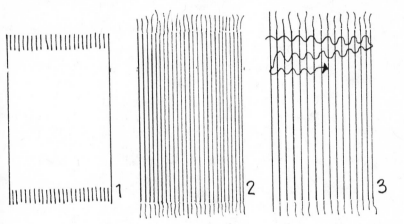

SAND PAINTING:

Take three or more plastic containers of sand.   Use dry powder paint to color sand in each container a different hue.   Children draw a picture on a piece of cardboard.   They mark off sections which are to be a different color.   Taking one section at a time, they apply Elmer's glue and then sprin- kle correct color of sand.   Let dry.   Repeat with each sec- tion.

TV BOX:

Objective: Construct a TV box to use for showing still frame pictures created by the children.

Materials: Cardboard box approximately 18" x 18" x 12" and a broomstick (4 feet) cut in half.

Directions: Take a cardboard box, remove the flaps on one side, and in the center of the opposite side cut a hole approximately 8 1/2" x 11 1/2". Near the face of the opening, on the adjoining short sides of the box, cut four holes for the broomstick poles as shown below.

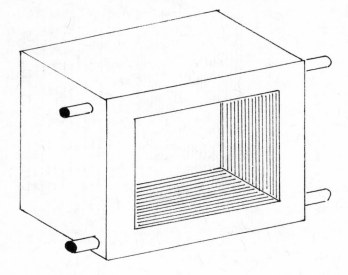

CHECK-IN POSTER:

Objective: To construct a durable poster for use by the children to check themselves in upon arrival in the morning.

Materials: Large, heavy cardboard sheet approximately 36" x 48" or larger; lightweight screw hooks numbering

five times the number of children in the room; 15 feet of
heavy packing tape (to reinforce the edges).

Directions: On the finished side of the cardboard sheet,
lay out the chart as shown. In each square of the chart,
gently screw in a hook in the top center of square.

Check-in

Name	M.	T.	W.	Th.	F.
John Adams	○	·	·	·	·
Sue Bye	·	○	·	·	·
Jane Carroll	·	○	·	·	·
etc.	·	○	·	·	·

Appendix D

RECOMMENDED LINGUISTIC READING PROGRAMS

Linguistic Reading Program	Supplementary Readers	Other Materials

Merrill Linguistic Readers
   Charles E. Merrill Pub.
   Co.
   Columbus, Ohio 43216
	Literature Ap-
	preciation Kit
	($45.00)
		Workbooks,
		Duplicating
		Masters

SRA Basic Reading Series
   Science Research Asso-
     ciates
   259 E. Erie Street
   Chicago, Illinois 60611
	BRS Satellites
	($42.50)
		Workbooks

Programmed Reading Text-
books
   Webster Division,
   McGraw Hill Book Co.
   St. Louis, Missouri
	Storybooks 1,
	1A, 1B to 14B.
	(Hardcovers;
	$1.50 per sto-
	rybook)
		Internal
		self-tests
		every 24
		pages.

Programmed Reading Text-
books (Remedial)
   Behavioral Research
     Laboratory
   Box 577
   Palo Alto, California
	Storybooks 1,
	1A, 1B to 12B.
	($1.00 per sto-
	rybook)
		Placement
		tests, Prog-
		ress tests,
		Sullivan
		Reading
		Games

Miami Linguistic Readers
   D. C. Heath & Co.
   School Division
   125 Spring Street
   Lexington, Mass. 02173

Primary Phonics Storybooks (1-25) (40¢ each)
   Educators Publishing Service, Inc.

75 Moulton Street
Cambridge, Mass.   02138

Stern: Structural Reading Series (Workbooks)
  Random House, Inc.
  457 Madison Ave.
  New York 22, New York

Durrell-Murphy: Speech-to-Print Phonics
                 Phonics Practice Program
  Harcourt, Brace, and World, Inc.
  1372 Peachtree Street, N.E.
  Atlanta, Georgia   30309

Sullivan Reading Games (Kit)
  Behavioral Research Laboratory
  Box 577
  Palo Alto, California

Sullivan Language Readiness (6 Big Books for teaching basic
  concepts, the alphabet, beginning reading skills. $200.00
  for the set.   Sold only as a set.) Behavioral Research
  Laboratory.

Bereiter and Englemann: "Music for Language Development"
  (Chapter 9), Teaching the Disadvantaged Child.   Engle-
  wood Cliffs, N.J.: Prentice-Hall, 1966.   (The songs
  have also been produced as a box of records.) ($50.00)

Big Books: Getting Ready to Read (2 volumes); Learning
  Letter Sounds (Well programmed for teaching letter-sound
  relations.) Houghton Mifflin Co., 666 Miami Circle, N.E.,
  Atlanta, Georgia   30324

Spin and Spell Word Making Games, Set 1 ($1.50).   Philo-
  graph Publication Ltd., Fulham, London, England

The New Linguistic Block Series 1L:SPELL ($10.50) (with
  workbook).   Linguistic Block Series: Rolling Phonics --
  VOWELS. Scott, Foresman & Co., 433 East Erie Street,
  Chicago 11, Illinois

TAKE, A Sound Matching Game ($1.75); POPPER WORDS
  (group size) Set 1 - First 110 of the Dolch 220 Basic
  Service Words ($2.00); Set 2 - Second 110 of the Dolch
  220 Basic Service Words ($2.00). Garrard Press,
  Champaign, Illinois

Phonic Rummy, card sets A, B, C, D, Games of Matching
  Sounds ($1.75). Junior Phonic Rummy, A Reading Game
  of Short Vowel Words for Beginning Reading ($1.75).

You Can Read: Phonetic Drill Cards. Kenworthy Educational Service, Inc., Buffalo, New York

Phonetic Word Builder ($1.75). Milton Bradley, 74 Park
  Street, Springfield, Mass. 01105

Alphasets (2 and 3 inch multiple felt-backed durable cardboard letters). 2" upper case letters and numerals; 2"
  lower case letters ($3.50 each box). 3" upper case let-
  ters and numerals; 3" lower case letters ($3.95 each box)

CONTRACTS

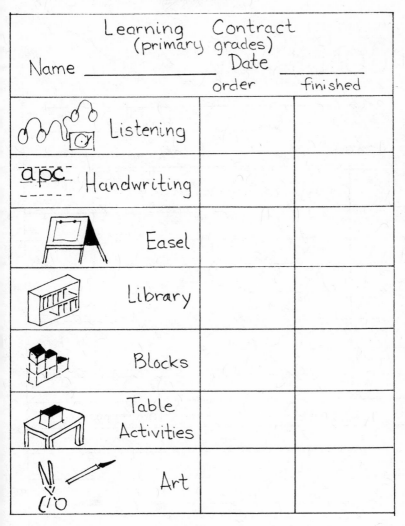

Learning Contract (primary grades)		
Name _____ Date _____	order	finished
Listening		
Handwriting		
Easel		
Library		
Blocks		
Table Activities		
Art		

(intermediate grades)

Work Study
CONTRACT
For:_____

Today's date: _____

Approved by:_____ Date:_____

Job No.	Type of work/study	Date Due

Unfinished Work for Tomorrow

RECOMMENDED BOOKS

Resources for projects, teaching tips, etc.

Campbell, David. A Practical Guide to the Open Classroom.
University of Pittsburgh Press, 1971.

Collier, Mary Jo, Imogen Forte, and Joy MacKenzie. Kid's
Stuff. Nashville, Tennessee: Incentive Publications, Inc.,
1969.

Craig, Gerald S. Science for the Elementary School Teacher.
Ginn and Company, 1966.

Edgren, Harry D. and Joseph J. Gruber. Teacher's Handbook of Indoor and Outdoor Games. Prentice-Hall, Inc.,
1963.

Grade Teacher Magazine--clip articles of interest and make
a notebook of project ideas by subject.

Holt, John. What Do I Do On Monday. E. P. Dutton and
Company, 1970.

Hurwitz, Abraham, and Arthur Goddard. Games to Improve
Your Child's English. Simon and Schuster, 1969.

Leeper, Sarah Hammond, Ruth Dales, Dora Skipper and
Ralph Witherspoon. Good School for Young Children.
Macmillan Co., 1968.

Shape and Size, Pictorial Representation, I Do and I Under-
stand, Computations and Structure, Mathematics Begins,
New York: John Wiley and Sons, Inc., for the Nuffield
Foundation.

134 The Open Classroom

Sharp, Evelyn. Thinking Is Child's Play. E. P. Dutton and Company, 1969.

Resources for Theory

Ashton-Warner, Sylvia. Teacher. Simon and Schuster, 1963.

Dennison, George. The Lives of Children. Random House, 1969.

Engelmann, Siegfried. Preventing Failure in the Primary Grades. Simon and Schuster, 1969.

Gattegno, Caleb. What We Owe Children: The Subordination of Teaching to Learning. Outerbridge and Dienstfrey, 1970.

Herndon, James. How to Survive in Your Native Land. Simon and Schuster, 1971.

Holt, John. How Children Learn. Pitman, 1967.

Kohl, Herbert. The Open Classroom. Pitman, 1967.

Kozol, Jonathan. Death at an Early Age. Houghton-Mifflin Company, 1967.

Lembo, John M. Why Teachers Fail. Columbus, Ohio: Charles E. Merrill Publishing Co., 1971.

Postman, Neil and Charles Weingartner. Teaching as a Subversive Activity. Delacorte Press, 1969.

Rotzel, Grace. The School in Rose Valley. Johns Hopkins Press, 1971.

Silberman, Charles E. Crisis in the Classroom. Random House, 1970.

_____. The Open Classroom Reader. Random House, 1973.

Weber, Evelyn. Early Childhood Education: Perspectives on Change. Charles A. Jones Publishing Co., 1970.

Weber, Lillian. The English Infant School and Informal Education. Prentice-Hall, Inc., 1971.

Appendix F   135

Activities for Learning Centers

Croft, Doreen J. and Robert D. Hess. An Activities Hand-
    book for Teachers of Young Children. New York: Hough-
    ton Mifflin, 1972.

Farallones Scrapbook: Making Places, Changing Spaces in
    Schools at Home and Within Ourselves. Random House,
    Inc., 1971.

Idea Book for Learning Centers. Kings Park/Kings Glen
    Elementary School, Fairfax County, Virginia, 1970.

Learning Centers: Children on Their Own. Association for
    Childhood Education International., 3615 Wisconsin Ave.,
    N.W., Washington, D. C. 20016. $2.00/copy.

Rogers, Vincent R. Teaching in British Primary Schools.
    New York: The MacMillan Co., 1970.

Spache, Evelyn B. Reading Activities for Child Involvement.
    Boston: Allyn and Bacon, Inc., 1972.

Spice: A Handbook of Activities to Motivate Teaching of
    Elementary Language Arts. Stevensville, Michigan: Edu-
    cational Service, 1960.

Thompson, Richard A. Energizers for Reading Instruc-
    tion. West Nyack, New York: Parker Publishing Co.,
    Inc., 1973.

INDEX

ability groups 5
achievement, individual 70, 78, 84, 91, 102
   reading 66
activities
   clean-up 22
   free choice of 23, 24, 25, 29, 31
   language arts 19, 20, 24, 28, 30, 31, 32, 36, 39, 43,
      44, 63, 107, 108, 111, 113, 114, 115, 116, 117, 118,
      128
   lists of 30, 35, 36, 37, 57, 63, 79, 85, 107-116
   math 20, 23, 28, 29, 30, 31, 36, 37, 39, 42, 43, 63,
      108, 109, 120
   miscellaneous 16, 19, 20, 26, 30, 31, 32, 33, 36, 64,
      107, 108, 109, 110, 111, 112, 125
   music 16, 19, 20, 26, 30, 31, 32, 33, 36, 64, 107,
      108, 109, 110, 111, 112, 125
   reading 19, 20, 24, 28, 30, 31, 32, 43, 45, 46, 63,
      107, 108, 109, 112, 113, 114, 115, 116, 117, 118,
      119
   science 20, 30, 32, 36, 37, 63, 78, 110, 111, 116
   social studies 18, 23, 30, 32, 36, 37, 110, 111
   structured 18-23, 31, 35, 60
activity cards 38, 80
   examples of 39
activity checklist 25
administration 1, 33, 34, 93
administrative duties 13
advantages of open education 1
afternoon activity period: chpt. 3 65, 69, 82
afternoon schedule 29, 31, 32, 65
alternatives to present education 1
arrival at school 13, 59, 63, 102, 126
art activities 30, 32, 36, 37, 47, 63, 107, 110, 114, 115,
     124, 125
art center 47, 50, 71, 73, 76
assigning groups 18
assignments, specific 5, 13

DATE DUE

MAR 2 '78 MAY 19 '79			
MAR 30 '79 MAR 20 '79			
APR 11 '79 APR 11 '79			
MAR 27 '80 MAR 27 '80			
APR 17 '80 APR 17 '80			
MAY 6 ' MAY 6 '82			
APR 15 '81 APR 16 '81			
AP 7 '82 APR 8 '82			
AP 9 '84 APR 2 '84			
GAYLORD			PRINTED IN U.S.A